T0328509

Literature, Literary Criticism and National Development

Malthouse Critical Works

Literature, Literary Criticism and National Development

Professor Charles E. Nnolim

Former Dean, Faculty of Humanities
University of Port Harcourt,
Port Harcourt, Nigeria.

Malthouse Press Limited

Lagos, Benin, Ibadan, Jos, Port-Harcourt, Zaria

© C.E. Nnolim 2016
First Published 2016
ISBN 978-978-53250-8-9

Published by
Malthouse Press Limited
43 Onitana Street, Off Stadium Hotel Road,
Surulere, Lagos, Lagos State
E-mail: malthouse_press@yahoo.com
malthouselagos@gmail.com
www.malthouselagos.com
Tel: +234 (0)802 600 3203

Dedication

To,

Mr Simon alagbogu Nnolim who sent me to school but wanted me, above all things, to be a policeman. Brother dear, sorry I did not meet your wishes because I lacked the height. but see what I have made of myself with the height God has given me.

and

To my mother, Mrs Angelina Lolo Nnolim, Ada Ezelibe, who worked and starved and 'shielded' me from farm work so I could go to school

Foreword

Despite my decade and a half long relationship with Professor Charles E. Nnolim, it came as a pleasant surprise and honour to me that I would be asked to write a foreword to this book of essays. This is more so when this is probably what our respected Professor would consider as his substantive post-retirement book and programmatic statement on what he considers his service to literature. It is equally exciting to note that Professor Charles Nnolim right at the time of commissioning this assignment was prepared to wait for roughly six months for this "Foreword" to be written. For an intellectual who has become celebrated as Fellow Nigerian Academy of Letters, Fellow, World Academy of Letters, Laureate of Nigerian National Order of Merit and distinguished lecturer at the Nigerian National Merit Award among others, it is a great honour to be requested to do the present job.

Contrary to the impression created by Charles Nnolim in *Approaches to the African Novel: Essays in Analysis.* (1992) and his responses to three interview questions posed by the present writer in *Reconstructing the Canon: Festschrift in Honour of Professor Charles Nnolim,* the 'social use of literature' which ordinarily should be anathema to a formalist literary critic is ironically the main focus of the collection of essays compiled in the present book, *Literature, Literary Criticism and National*

Development. However, it is salutary that in responding to this writer's query about whether one can "talk about literary criticism without relating it to (ideal of the) common welfare," Charles Nnolim notes that "we do so at our own peril. It is common welfare that forms the background of both literature and its criticism" *(Reconstructing* 54). Furthermore, after isolating variables whose essence he associates with the common welfare (poetic justice, morality, religion, good and bad literature), Nnolim volunteers that "there is no way we can talk about literary criticism without drawing attention to the human dimensions or the way literature affects the lives of men and women *(Reconstructing* 54-55).

It is quite intriguing that after all the sky-bound arguments in the rather exclusive and exotic literary journals, Charles E. Nnolim would in these essays originally delivered as public lectures come down to the level of those who may be ordinary literary enthusiasts and outside the constituency of the Rene Welleks, Frank Kermodes, Northrop Fryes and so on. In assembling these essays in the present book, Nnolim is following in the footsteps of, among others, Frank Kermode whose *The Genesis of Secrecy* his engagement with the literary construction of the Bible is derived from his Norton lectures. It is the same way in which Kermode's *History and Value* (1988) is a product of 'five series of lectures' (Michael Payne 13). And nearer home he joins the league of Femi Osofisan of *Literature and the pressures of freedom* (2001).

These lectures delivered at significant points in Professor Nnolim's career, mark his academic growth and deepening awareness of the role of literature in national development. *Literature and the Common Welfare* (1988) was his inaugural lecture, his declaration that he had come of age as an academic, as a young Professor of literature. In

August 2000, he delivered the lecture *Literature, the Arts and Cultural Development,* a command lecture, to announce his induction as a member of the Nigerian Academy of Letters in which he was finally investitured as fellow in 2005. In this lecture, Nnolim makes strong claims about the validity of literature in Nigeria's national life:

> Our literatures have indeed fostered national consciousness, patriotism, and nationalism. Every Nigerian holds his head high anywhere in the world because Achebe, Okara, Soyinka, Ola Rotimi, Niyi Osundare, Festus Iyayi, Ken Saro Wiwa and Ben Okri are indigenes of this country of literary giants. Nigeria's most valued export commodity is not petroleum products but her literatures which have won every imaginable international prize including the Nobel-prize...Through her literatures... Nigeria exports her culture and tradition to other parts of the world and, through these literary works exposes to the world the very foundations of her national consciousness (23).

In August, 2007, Nnolim had the duty to deliver another "command" lecture in the third University of Port Harcourt School of Graduate Studies Public Lecture series entitled: *The Writer's Responsibility and Literature in National Development.* Here Nnolim re-emphasizes, indeed repeats the importance of literary studies in Nigeria's national life but goes on to lament the total neglect of our artists, writers, and world class intellectuals in our national life. He argues:

> Achebe in his Nigerian National Order of Merit lecture captioned "What Has Literature Got to do with it" tells us that a nation becomes what it honours and how it does it is a paradigm of its national style. Nigeria does not even pretend to honour knowledge in the same way it regularly honours its politicians through public monuments...Nigeria which has never batted an eyelid in building houses and naming streets after mere teenage footballers, has never seen it fit to extend that

sort of courtesy to our eminent writers and world-class intellectuals. (37)

Morning Yet on Criticism Day: the Criticism of African Literature in the Twentieth Century is yet another "command" lecture required of Nnolim as a laureate of the Nigerian National Merit Award, 2009. It unifies Professor Nnolim's various pleas for the role of literature in national development by further underlining ideas advanced in these lectures but particularly re-emphasizing the problem of language in Nigeria's creative writing and urging governmental intervention in the matter.

Austin Amanze Akpuda
Abia State University

Contents

Ridentem Dicere Verum:
Literature and the Common Welfare [*]

"And what are you reading Miss ----?" "Oh! it is only a novel" replies the young lady; while she lays down her book with affective indifference, or momentary shame. "It is only *Cecilia* or *Camilia* or *Belinda,* or, in short, only some work in which the greatest powers of the mind are displayed, in which the most thorough knowledge of human nature, the happiest delineations of its varieties, the liveliest effusions of wit and humour, are conveyed to the world in the best chosen language."

(Jane Austen: *Northanger Abbey)*

Those of us raised in the rural environment, as most of us were, might have observed that little dance (which looks like a threat) which the cock does toward the hen after riding her and climbing down from her back. "I will buy you the long Akwette cloth" it promises the hen, according to our elders. "Promises, promises", the hen is said to invariably reply, distrustingly. The kid goat, in another incident observed by our elders, is once said to have packed bag and baggage to go and seek out a wife. The mother naturally opposed the trip. The kid-goat turns around and says: "Mother, if you don't

---

[*] An Inaugural Lecture Delivered At The University Of Port Harcourt July 13, 1988, University Of Port Harcourt1988

permit me to go out and find a wife, I will marry you!" And with that, he made very threatening passes at his mother.

The above are instructive. La Fontaine tells us: "I use animals to instruct men." In other words, literature, whether written or oral, is an expansion of the proverb. The cock may not have been making endless unfulfilled promises to the hen, *but it seems so*. And the kid goat may make threatening passes at his mother, but may not have threatened to marry her; *but it seems so*. When, therefore, the proverb is expanded, we are catapulted into another world of appearance and reality. And the world of appearance and reality is the very stuff of which literature is made. Once we enter into the realm of literature, we are catapulted according to Sister Sweeney, into another world, another country. In that world; through the powers of imagination, we are enabled:

> To see the world in a grain of sand
> And a heaven in a wild flower,
> Hold infinity in the palm of your hand
> And eternity in an hour
> (Blake.' Auguries of Innocence)

In the light of the above, for the next hour or so therefore, 1 invite you to accompany me on a visit to another country, a better land where things are better arranged than the one in which we at present find ourselves. But you have to be an alert guest or you will be like a traveller carried through a fascinating country full of beautiful and breathtaking landscapes, but fast asleep in a corner seat in your train. I invite you, therefore, to enter with me, the world of literature, and to enter this world is to willingly agree to submit yourself to be *deceived,* to accept the experience of a world where "flowers smile in the sunshine", and the night "approaches on bended knees before a moon-blanched evening". This is what that inimitable poet of eerie and surreal experience, Samuel Taylor Coleridge, aptly terms that "willing suspension of disbelief which constitutes poetic faith". An adult who accepts and enjoys the world of literature is like an old man who willingly joins children in a game of blind man's buff.

But before we sit pretty in this new world of literature, it is only proper that for those who are not quite sure of what it is, or have forgotten what it is supposed to be, their mind is refreshed. I define imaginative literature as that writing which is more emotionally moving than intellectually instructive; that writing which primarily deals with a make-believe world, whose language is highly connotative rather than denotative, symbolic rather than literal, figurative rather than plain; and whose ultimate aim is to produce a satisfyingly aesthetic effect and find anchor as a work of art. In its common categorizations, poetry, drama, and narrative fiction (the novel, the short story, the essay) belong to the major genres of belles-lettres. The ultimate test of literature as a "verbal work of art" is its *fictionality* and its *imaginative* import. Literature is an idea, a philosophy wrapped up in a symbol, an image, a concept. It is a performance in words: like a dance, it is full of intricate rhythms; like the masked spirit, it is full of mysteries.

But why literature? How does it conduce to our common welfare - the welfare of the individual and the welfare of society at large? How can literature help man cope with the business of life which is generally harsh? This is the burden of today's lecture. On the individual level, literature exists to open up for us the inner life of at least one other human being. By having glimpses into the inner lives of various other people, literature informs us of some of the resources of the human mind and spirit; of man's ability to love, hate, scheme; of his triumphs, ambitions, and frustrations; of his complexities and perversities "I owe everything to poetry", asserts Maurice de Guerin:

> I owe to it whatever I have pure, lofty' and solid in my soul; I owe to it all my consolation in the past; I shall probably owe to it my future *(Reliquiae).*

The above makes high claims for literature, on a personal level, for P. B. Shelley claims that "poetry is the record of the best and happiest moments, of the best and happiest minds," and that "poetry turns all things to loveliness; it exalts the beauty of that which is most beautiful and it adds beauty to that which is most deformed" *(A Defence of poetry).*

Maurice de Guerin must be right. He must have agreed with Shelley that "a poet is a nightingale who sits in darkness and sings to cheer its own solitude with sweet sounds: his auditors are men entranced by the melody of an unseen musician". Yes, poetry is a lovely song sung to delight and cheer men - to cheer us. The pleasure which only literature or poetry can offer begins with the arrangement of words into pleasurable patterns - what has been referred to as the right words in the right order", or as Alexander Pope might say, it consists in

> What oft was thought?
> But ne'er so well expressed

Listen to the pleasure derived in the arrangement of words into what we commonly refer to as alliteration or tongue twisters:

> Peter piper picked a peck of pickled pepper A peck of pickled pepper peter piper picked If peter piper picked a peck of

pickled pepper Where's the peck of pickled pepper Peter Piper picked.

Or this

Mrs. Butter went to buy some better butter To make her bitter butter better

We also read poetry for its melody, for the rhythm it offers. Listen to this rhythmic piece meant for children's enjoyment:

Pretty little song bird
Happy as a king
Will you tell me truly
Why is it you sing
Early in the morning
At the break of the day
High up in the blue sky
In sweet tones I pray
I praise God the father
Every time I sing
And then pay my homage
To the great high king

Literature, as we can see is both poetry and music, and both exist to entertain us, to offer us pleasure: the pleasure we derive from listening to good music. And Shakespeare tells us in *The Merchant of Venice:*

That man that hath no music in himself
Nor is not moved with concord of sweet sounds.
Is fit for treasons, stratagems, and spoils;
The motion of his spirit are dull as night
And his affections dark as Erebus
Let no such man be trusted.

I have said that Maurice de Guerin must be right, for literature exists to please, to lighten the burden of men's lives, to make us forget for a short while our sorrows and disappointments in life; to help us face our frustrations and uncertain futures. Matthew Arnold characteristically assigns a noble function to poetry, to literature:

> We should conceive of poetry worthily, and more highly than it has been the custom to conceive of it. We should conceive of it as capable of higher uses, and called to higher destinies, than those which in general men have assigned to it hitherto. More and more mankind will discover that we have to turn to poetry to interpret life for us, to console us, to sustain us. Without poetry our science will appear incomplete; and most of what now passes with us for religion and philosophy will be replaced by poetry *(The study of poetry)*.

We must therefore agree that literature makes definite contributions to human knowledge. We, therefore, read literature because all knowledge is naturally agreeable to us, and if, as in most literatures, that knowledge is imparted interestingly, it provides a pleasant truce from our cares. Literature, by expanding our intellectual horizons allows us to imbibe certain seeds of wisdom in the process. And an acquisition of knowledge and wisdom is an acquisition of happiness, for good literature, like good art, creates for man the highest enjoyment.

Moreover, good literature sharpens our aesthetic sensibilities for the appreciation of the beautiful. Didn't Robert Browning say in "Fra Lippo Lippi":

> If you get simple beauty and naught else.
> You get about the best thing God invents

Literature thus produces desirable effects on the reader

by means of the aesthetic experience it evokes. And a good aesthetic experience not only does no one any harm but relieves tensions and suppresses destructive impulses, thus resolving lesser conflicts within us and helping to create an integration or harmony within the self. Bertrand Russell in his Nobel Prize acceptance speech had claimed that the love of excitement is one of the fundamental motives of man — the excitement of invention or artistic creation and the excitement of discovery including the discovering and exploration of a new complex work of art which, according to him, are two of the highest, purest, satisfying types of excitement. This tonic effect which art and literature provide, always creates a pleasant diversion for a troubled mind.

At the level of society, the aesthetic experience fosters mutual sympathy and understanding and, according to Munroe Beardsley *(The Inherent Value of Art)*, will help, on a larger scale, to draw men together, since all shared experience helps to bring people together in friendship and mutual respect, for any group of people who share the same aesthetic experience, have a bond between them; any group of persons who share the joys which only literature can give never feel emptiness, frustration, lack of fulfilment or despair-feelings that cripple the mind.

As we have seen, literature reconciles groups of people through shared experience. It does more: it teaches us about life while it both entertains and offers us aesthetic enjoyment. Every short story, every novel, every poem, every drama worth its salt as a work of art, has a thing or two to say about life, has a moral view of life it enunciates, has a philosophy of life that it imparts. A study of various works of literature is, in fact, a study of various philosophies of life, for every author implants a little stamp of his philosophy in his story, novel, poem, drama. Take Shakespeare's *Macbeth*.

What does it say about life. It is embedded in that famous passage which reads:

> Tomorrow, and tomorrow, and tomorrow,
> Creeps in this petty pace from day to day
> To the last syllable of recorded time
> And all our yesterdays have lighted fools
> The way to dusty death. Out, out, brief candle!
> Life's but a walking shadow, a poor player
> That struts and frets his time upon the stage
> And then is heard no more: it is a tale
> Told by an idiot, full of sound and fury,
> Signifying nothing.

What does this passage Say about life and about Macbeth? It talks about the futility of unbridled ambition. It asks what a man like Macbeth, as well as his wife, has gained from life by achieving the throne by way of murder and blood: unhappiness, a terribly guilty conscience, blood-stained hands, sleeplessness, a besmirched reputation, an abysmally empty life with nagging nightmares, an awareness of the futility of it all. Only fools seek such lives that mean no more than appearances. And Macbeth and his wife were such arch fools.

Nearer home Achebe from one important work to another makes a significant statement about life: that no one can successfully resist the forces of change, because the forces of change are by far stronger than the stubborn individual. So, Okonkwo, and Ezeulu, and Teacher Nanga are swept away by the strong current of the forces of change. According to Achebe, then, the prudent man must go along, even if grudgingly, and change with the times.

If we agree with Matthew Arnold that literature is "capable of higher uses and called to higher destinies" and that "we have to turn to poetry to interpret life for us, to console us, to sustain us; we shall appreciate the more the interpretive value of Leigh Hunt's celebrated humanist poem, *Abou Ben Adhem,* which reminds us of Christ's answer to the lawyer who demanded to know the greatest of God's commandments. Christ had answered him: "Love the lord thy God with thy whole heart, with thy whole mind, and with thy whole soul. And the second is like unto the first: Love thy neighbour as thyself' *Abou Ben Adhem* is thus a poem that restates Christ's answer in a humanistic way by saying that love of man can indeed save you more than the mere abstract love of God. For how can we claim to love God whom we don't see if we don't love our *fellow* men whom we see. The parable of the Good Samaritan which answers with such clarity the question of "who is my neighbour" is thus given a refreshingly new twist in Leigh Hunt's poem. Here is the poem:

Abou Ben Adhem

ABOU *BEN* ADHEM, may his tribe increase!
Awoke one night from a *deep* dream of peace,
And saw, within the moonlight in his room,
Making it rich and like a lily in bloom,
An angel writing in a book of gold.

Exceeding peace had made Ben Adhem bold,
And to the presence in the room he said,
What writest thou?' - The Vision raised its head,
And with a look made of all sweet accord,
Answered: The names of those who love the Lord!

`And is mine one?' said Abou. 'Nay, not so'.
Replied the angel. Abou spoke more low
But cheerly still, said, 'I pray thee then,
Write me as one that loves his fellow men'.

The angel wrote and vanished. The next night
It came again with a great wakening light,
And showed the names whom love of God had blessed.
And lo! Ben Adhem's name led all the rest.

In sum, literature acts as *aids* to life, like prayers that, in Mattthew Arnold's words, are there "to sustain us", and give inspiration and courage to the despairing so that (to quote Arnold one more time) "most of what now passes with us for religion and philosophy will be replaced by poetry." Take William Ernest Henley's famous *Invictus*. Henley (R. L. Stevenson's prototype for Long John Silver in *Treasure Island)*, contracted cancer of the bone at the age of twelve. One leg had been amputated, and doctors had recommended the amputation of the other one, (Henley had refused and stoically bore the agony throughout life (he died in his fifties). The following poem, *Invictus* (unconquered) is what he wrote to inspire his courage throughout life:

Out of the night that covers me,
Black as the Pit from pole to pole,
I thank whatever gods may be
For my unconquerable soul.
In the fell clutch of circumstances
I have not winced nor cried aloud
Under the bludgeonings of chance
My head is bloody, but unbowed.

Beyond this place of wrath and tears
Looms but the horror of the shade,
And yet the menace of the years
Finds, and shall find, me unafraid.

It matters not how straight the gate
How charged with punishments the scroll,
I am the master of my fate:
I am the captain of my soul.

Literature thus offers admonition and advice on how to bear the vagaries of life, how to cope with the agony of existence in a world of generally missed opportunities. We are all used to the self defeating adage that "opportunity occurs but once". But Walter Malone in a famous poem urges us to disregard this self-defeating adage and, instead, tells us to take courage because opportunity does in fact present itself again and again in our lives. His poem which was set to music and entitled "Opportunity" reads:

They do me wrong who say I come no more,
When once I come and fail to find you in,
For everyday I stand outside your door,
And bid you wake and rise to fight and win.

Wail not for precious chances passed away,
Weep not for golden ages on the wane,
Each night I burn the records of the day,
At sunrise every soul is born again
{I cannot do it never accomplishes anything I'll try had done wonders).

Where else do we go for uplifting advice as above but to literature. Have you forgotten Douglas Malloch?:

If you can't be a pine on top of a hill
Be a scrub in the Valley but be
The best little scrub by the side of the rill...
Be the best of whatever you are

And Rudyard Kipling:

If you can keep your head when all about you
Are losing theirs and blaming it on you
If you can trust yourself when all men doubt you
But make allowance for their doubting too

If you can wait and not be tired waiting
Yours is the earth and everything that's in it
And which is more — you'll be a man, my son!

Even in death, literature does not abandon us but tries to reconcile us to the fact of death by trying to cushion the impact as an event sweetly anticipated, for finally laying down quietly our weary, old bones. Listen to Spenser's anodyne:

Sleep after toyle, port after stormie seas,
Ease after wane, death after life, does greatly please (Spenser:
The Faerie Queene)

There are other uses of literature to which we have not called attention. Literature records man's infinite desire for the unattainable, for what Shelley calls, "the desire of the moth for a star." Man's longing for a perfect society, a society where all his problems have been solved, a paradise on earth, has bred a sub-genre of works popularly known as "Utopian Literature." Plato originated this sub-genre in the Republic, but Thomas More's Utopia (coined from two Greek words "Outopia" (no place) and "Eutopia" (the good place), meaning "the good place is no place", gave it its generic nomenclature. In utopian literature, the wretched of the earth who unhappily find themselves in this valley of tears are invited to partake, even if vicariously, of the kingdom idea, full of the delights and satisfactions denied them in this harsh world of reality. Utopian literature, therefore, is mainly a literature of escape because, the kernel of the sub-genre contains man's longing for a world where man's problems have already been solved and the tears of suffering humanity have completely been wiped dry.

Now, to deny that man needs promise of a better future to exist is to deny man's basic longing for a future of satisfactions and fulfilment — to pose hell for him instead of heaven for all his deprivations, privations, hard work and struggles, and that would tantamount to denial of the truth of the essence of man's existence. We need utopian literature to fulfil man's anticipatory longing for a reward for his labours, for rest after his toils, for transformation of an earthly kingdom into a heavenly kingdom:" According to Paul Tillich (in "Critique and Justification of Utopia"), there are two main characteristics of utopia: its power and its fruitfulness. Its power builds on man's ontological discontent with his lot in life forcing man to break from this ontological discontent in order to transform his dreams into reality, and also its ability to open up possibilities for man which would have remained lost to him if not envisaged by utopian anticipation of human fulfilment. The fruitfulness of utopia becomes the many realizations by man of his dreams on earth through his inventive genius and scientific discoveries that made possible a constantly dynamic present that keeps breaking into a better-realized future.

For those of us in the humane letters who read the Bible as the Judaic literary legacy to the world, the Bible is utopian literature *par excellence,* depicting for mankind a visionary anticipation of the coming kingdom under God, the millennia at the end of time which is apocalyptic. By prophecy, by sheer intense if fanatical imaginative projection, the Israelites were able to break out from the slavery which was Egypt, to attainment of the Promised Land which was Jerusalem. The realization of the Jewish dream is proof of the power of utopia.

The above must of necessity force us to reflect on the place of utopian literature on the African scene. While the European concept of utopia is futuristic, reflecting a future-oriented world-view, African concept of utopia is, in the main, backward-looking, reflecting a backward-looking world view.

We would easily agree that the legacy of Europe and the West is the legacy of a universe which continues to be transformed through outstanding scientific and technological break-through. Why is this? Europe and the West are societies which make the problems of the future their centre of interest today. Read Jules Verne's *From the Earth to the Moon* (he predicted a journey to the moon from a rocket launched from Cape Canaveral. It was so accomplished one hundred later). Alvin Toffler's *Future Shock* with futuristic as insistence that we should be "educating for ", "preparing people for the future", and his warning that "unless man quickly learns to control the rate of change in his personal affairs as well as in society at large, we are doomed to a massive adaptational breakdown!". Archibald Macleish had written in "America was Promises":

America was always promises
From the first voyage and the first ship There were promises.

And Bellamy in *Looking Backward* tells us:

Looking Backward was written in the belief that the Golden Age lies before us and not behind us, and is not far away. Our children shall surely see it, and we, too, who are already men and women, if we deserve it by our faith and by our work.

While science fiction which is, in the main, futuristic, crowds modern fiction-writing in Europe thus ensuring a more scientific, technologically-oriented future for Europe and the West, African utopia continues to be backward-looking. As Ivor Case puts it succinctly, in African traditional religions:

There is no prophetism and no future paradise. For time...
recedes rather than progresses and the Golden Age — that era
of the black man's greatness — the era of Timbuctoo and
Benin, the era of the Yoruba and the Zulu, of Shango and
Chaka, lies in the Zamani period. The Sasa is an ever constant
construction of the past and not of the future. Utopia exists in
the past ("Negritude and Utopianism")

The Negritude movement was African utopian literature
par excellence with its consistent *retour aux sources* or
return-to-the-sources theme. It was buttressed by the return
to Africa movement of Marcus Garvey, the Harlem
Renaissance in the U.S., Indigenism in Haiti, Afro-Cubanism
in Cuba, the Rastafarian Movement in Jamaica, and the cult
of primitivism in the Caribbean. Each, along with the
Negritude movement was a *retour aux sources* romantic
longing for the African past by writers for whom Africa
remained a lost paradise, to which we must all return for the
authentication of our humanity denied, debased, and
enslaved by the colonial masters. Alex Haley's *Roots*
becomes in recent times, the enthronement of the ex-slave's
longing for his place of origin. But nearer home, Chinua
Achebe indulges in ancestor worship while Camara Laye
returns imaginatively to his unspoilt childhood and unspoilt
Guinea; while the most celebrated return syndrome in
Caribbean literature is encapsulated in Cesaire's Cahier *d iin
Refour au pays natal (return to my native country)*.

As we can see, with all writers from Africa and of
African descent harping on a return to the past, to the womb
of time, where then is the shaping utopia for change in the
future, for a future paradise where African's present
problems are imaginatively solved? If it is true as Paul
Tillich asserts, that "for a culture which has no utopia the
present is inhibiting, the future holds no promise and the

danger is very much there... of falling back on its past", aren't there great and disturbing implications for Africa, since we now recognize the fact that the power of utopia consists in its ability to transform dreams into reality? And since we further recognize that utopian literature, when it is futuristic and forward-looking has made inventions possible, what happens to us and to Africa where no anticipatory utopia exists to open up possibilities for man? Does this imply for us, as Paul Tillich suggests, "a sterile present" where "not only individual but cultural realization of human possibilities are inhibited and remain unfulfilled?" The answer is not far to seek since we continue to send our best engineers and technologists to train in the effete factories in London when commonsense dictates that they trained in Japan whose innovative technology and technique of adapting other people's methods to suit her environment without destroying her culture, is the wonder of our modern technological age.

Since we, as Africans, do not project problems in the future and start to think of solving them now, it has not occurred to various African Governments including our own to embark on a massive exposure of our engineers and scientists to the wonder of Japan so that we may learn how Japan maintains an enviably buoyant economy while it imports 100 per cent of its oil needs and about 90 per cent of its steel requirement; how Japan has succeeded in beating the West at its own game. This lack of vision on our part has created enormous developmental problems for Africa.

I suggest that Africa's economic, developmental, and technological ills utopian literature can only be cured by a proper infusion of the right sort of utopian literature in our midst, stranger than fiction as this may seem. For example, Azania or South Africa is a land literally flowing with milk and honey, with its mines scintillating with gold and diamonds. But in spite of the brutalization, the degradation alienation, and exile they suffer at the hands of the whites, there is no sustained, prophetic, imaginative utopian future literature emanating from Black South Africa, projecting into the future a time of final home-coming or apocalyptic return of her scattered peoples to their promised New Jerusalem after the last white man must have been imaginatively driven into the sea.

Part of the burden of this lecture, then, is to call on African writers who should be her bearers of utopia, to effect a turn-about in their vision and challenge all of us by facing the future rather than dwelling in the pasts; by writing futuristic literature to redirect our vision and make all us forwarding-looking. The Negritude movement has run its course and, while it lasted, it had solved the problem of rehabilitating our essential humanity. I envisage that if our creative writers henceforth face the future through imaginative projection of our problems that are equally imaginatively solved, we shall have taken the first steps in solving Africa's developmental problems, today. Until our writers begin to depict Africa as a land of promise and project her as a continent with a great future, there will always be a worm that squirms at the core of her developmental plans which, as now, will always have an ad hoc, stop-gap syndrome that has hitherto stymied her long —range planning efforts. This is the challenge I pose.

But to leave the Negritude movement on this negative note is to be unfair to it catalytic effect on African literature. The Negritude movement was the centre-piece of Africa's literary nationalism which closely followed political nationalism in the wake of political independence for all black peoples. To regain cultural initiative, to imbue political independence with national and cultural pride, to embark on the path of psychic reconstruction, were what gave birth to the literary movement now known as Negritude, Negritude, what Jean Paul Sartre calls "an anti-racial racism" was embarked upon by writers of African descent as a form of literary therapy — for the common welfare of all people of African descent, even if surprised Europeans call the product of Negritude "sacrificing art to propaganda". So, all the back-to-the-sources movement I have earlier listed — Afro-Cubanism in Cuba, Indigenism in Haiti, the Harlem Renaissance in the U.S., nativism in West Africa — all these were roads, leading all peoples of African descent to recovering their essential self-hood bashed and mutilated by white arrogance through the colonial intrusion. The Negritude movement — that literary effort to conquer *blanchitude with Negritude* — was mass therapy, a home-coming of the prodigal to recover his essential self-hood. As I have said elsewhere, the essence of the Negritude movement consisted in its concern with

> the rehabilitation of the black man; in its stressing the innate dignity of the African personality; in its turning for inspiration in art and letters to African folk culture which, it insisted upon, was still a reservoir of the rhythm and lyricism of its poetry; in its insistence on the "felt" quality of the poetry of all African peoples; in its demonstration of the life-force that governs the art of all African peoples; and most importantly, in its encouragement of the study and appreciation of our African heritage.

If, then, the Negritude movement is an attempt by writers of African descent to domesticate literature for our own good, the language in which that literature is expressed becomes of primary importance if we shall not continue to talk of our common welfare in a foreign tongue. To assume a language, one critic has remarked, is to assume a world or, more explicitly, to assume a world-view. When Prospero (the imperial master) taught Caliban his language, he made sure his conquest of Caliban was complete. As George Lamming regretfully asserts,

> "provided there is no extraordinary departure which explodes all of Prospero' s premises, then Caliban and his future now belong to Prospero... Prospero lives in the absolute certainty that language, which is his gift to Caliban, is the very prison in which Caliban's achievements will be realized and restricted."

Sad as it seems, we are the calibans of literary history and the European imperialist is prospero. The single-handed battle being currently fought by Kenya's Ngugi wa Thiong'o to make his fellow contemporary African writers write in their indigenous languages may be unpopular and may presently fall on deaf ears, but it is the correct battle to fight, even if we admit it is at moment premature. In the long run, the decolonization of African literature will never be complete until the African writer is weaned from the linguistic and literary breast of Europe, until he no longer speaks to his people in an alien tongue. The domestication of the English language by African writers like Achebe by imposing Igbo speech patterns on the English language, while commendable, is not enough. Our common Welfare demands that we ultimately write our literature in our indigenous languages.

Mr. Vice-Chancellor, Sir, the pattern of Inaugural Lectures in this university have been for the lecturer to stress his own personal contribution to our own national welfare. Immodest as I have viewed this trend, I find justification for it in the lecturer's effort to deny that he is an ivory tower academic pontificating on abstract and high-falutin ideas that have little practical application. In the light of the above, let me immodestly repeat here, for the record, my own efforts to draw national attention to the contributions of literature to our common welfare as a nation.

As the current president of the Literary Society of Nigeria, I have had occasion to address the Federal Government on the need to champion the cause of literature because it conduces to the national welfare. In that address we told the Government, *inter alia* (c.f.: communiqué of the Conference of the Literary Society of Nigeria, A .B.U., March 1988):

(1) That Nigeria, through her literatures and her creative writers has won international attention and respect, not necessarily through science (which it sponsors) but through literature (which it spurns); that literature is perhaps, the one area in which Nigeria stands preeminent as the undisputed giant of Africa, in fact, of the entire Third World. Just last year Nigeria stood tall as her Wole Soyinka won the Nobel Prize for Literature, while Niyi Osundare won the Commonwealth poetry prize. In the light of the above, Nigeria's continued belief that the *materially relevant* discipline are of more relevance to our national needs, is a grand illusion;

(2) That the study of literature should be vigorously encouraged by the Federal Government at all levels of the educational system because literature as the expression of people's social consciousness and awareness has always performed an essential function in national development and is an important medium for the formulation and stabilization of positive social and cultural values;

(3) That literature affirms, through its progressive vision, the limitless possibilities of the human mind and thus inspires technological and scientific development by

inculcating visionary and positive values in the populace;

(4) That literature humanizes our otherwise science-dominated universe;

5) That through the process of social criticism literature influences the direction of national development and is a weapon for the total education of society because, our culture as a people is promoted, propagated and preserved in our national literatures whether vernacular, written or oral.

6) That in recognition of the above essential functions which literature performs and in order to ensure that these functions are performed with the best possible results, the Literary Society of Nigeria of which I am president urges Federal Government

a) to establish and fund a National Academy for the Humane Letters charged with popularizing and promoting our literatures;

b) to encourage the teaching of literature in all our schools by providing funds for research in the teaching of these subjects;

c) to fund the Literary Society of Nigeria and its organ, *Journal of the Literary Society of Nigeria*, which nurtures Nigeria's literary harvest;

d) to set up an institute charged with translating works written in various indigenous Languages into English, and works in English into these other languages;

(e) to encourage, improve, and promote the welfare of teachers of literature at all levels of our educational system;

(f) Finally, to ensure that the traditions of humane society which literature champions are entrenched in our national psyche through a proper education founded in the humanities because Nigeria through her literatures and her creative writers has won international acclaim and respect; and because literature humanizes our otherwise science-dominated universe

That these strident calls have fallen on deaf ears does not mean that we have not tried to urge public awareness of the place of literature in the welfare of our body-politic which is painfully full of materialistic philistines.

If we have thus stridently urged our various governments to more and more encourage the study of literature, it is because we also believe that literature has other higher uses than the merely mundane encouragement of national development. It is because we do not forget the higher uses of literature in the realm of ethics and morality. Tolstoy tells us (in What is art?):

> "Art is a human activity consisting in this, that one man consciously by means of certain external signs, hands on to others feelings he has lived through and that others are infected by these feelings and also experience them."

And T. S. Eliot adds (in "Religion and Literature") that "the author of a work of imagination is trying to affect us wholly, as human beings, whether he knows it or not; and we are affected by it, whether we intend to be or not."

Since the content of literature affects us, whether we like to be affected by it or not, it becomes imperative that in these times when our society is in a state of anomy and our youths are vulgarized, that our creative writers should concern themselves with moral and ethical issues in their works and produce good literature that *refines* and *uplifts* us instead of bad one that *vulgarizes* and *debases* us. T. S. Eliot further adds that "the greatness of literature cannot be determined solely by literary standards," because great literature, where it is worth the name, must be backed by great ethical and religious support, for great works of literature have been and "probably always will be judged by some moral standards." For our common welfare, therefore, it must be insisted that everything is not permissible. And since the issues of morality, of ethics, of good and evil cannot be avoided in our literatures the author who creates good and evil characters must tell us *where he stands.* Jeremy Collier admonishes us (in "A Short View of the Immorality and Profaneness of the English Stage"):

> The business of plays is to recommend virtue and discountenance vice, to show the uncertainty of human greatness, the sudden turns of fate and the unhappy conclusions of violence and injustice: It is to expose the singularities of pride and fancy, to make folly and falsehood contemptible, and to bring everything that is ill under infamy and neglect.

Ideas, they say, have legs, so that when an author creates evil characters and doesn't indicate to the reader where he stands by condemning or punishing him through poetic justice, he reverses (as one critic humorously put it) the words of Christ to the woman caught in adultery: he is telling the erring character: "neither do I condemn thee; go home and sin some more!" Fortunately, on the Nigerian literary scene, our most eminent writers — Achebe (in *No Longer At Ease* and A *Man of the People);* Soyinka (in *The Interpreters* and *A Season of Anomy);* and Okara (in *The Voice)* condemn their evil characters and insist that the onus of moral regeneration in our society lies with our intellectuals, as if in response to Nietzsche's call that "society needs an elite that will set a pattern and curb the thoughtlessness of the masses." So, Where Okara's Okolo becomes the voice of the elite crying in the wilderness for moral regeneration, Achebe's Odili becomes the same elite's voice in the political arena; but since he lacked the power base to effect the necessary correctives, the army had to come to his aid. The warning that our serious writers issue from one work to another is that nemesis overtakes both the populace and the rulers who abuse the system. On the other hand, one must condemn in very strong terms, writers like Dilibe Onyeama (in *Sex Is A Nigger's Game*) and other Nigerian purveyors of para-literature who lure our young readers into a world of sensual fantasy and mind-numbing drugs, thus watering the passions they should help to control.

Mr. Vice-Chancellor, Sir, we are about done. It remains for me to pull together the scattered strands of this discourse and perhaps nudge the audience into a clearer perception of the heart of the matter through a summary statement. Where else but through literature are we taught that life is a journey —from a narrow environment to a broader one, from childhood innocence to the wily ways of adulthood, from ignorance to experience, from naïveté to sophistication. Knowledge of the self and knowledge of the world and its ways is the one province of literature that is recognized above all others, for literature traces man undergoing several transitions, becoming more and more aware of things around him and adjusting to each environment at each stage of his development. The study of literature reveals that when man becomes incapable of adjustment, he becomes a tragic figure and goes the way of such fellows. The study of man is the province of literature Alexander Pope understood this perfectly when he said:

> Know thyself, presume not God to scan The proper study of mankind is man.

In studying mankind, we discover through literature that we must learn from the mistakes of other people who have suffered in life through misplaced ambitions, excessive jealousy, love of flattery, over-indulgence in worldly pleasures, since life is too short for anyone of us to learn all these things from his own mistakes. In tragedy, we see fellow men suffering because they rebelled against their own limitations. But this rebellion forces man, in his search for life's meaning, to come face to face with forces greater than he. We learn humility as we watch a greater man than ourselves go down, nobility and all, pride and all, fighting against a fatal stream that inevitably sweeps him along in its current.

But while tragedy deals with the rebellious spirit in man which is forcefully and painfully tamed by forces greater than man, comedy is concerned with the fact that despite our individual defeats, life does still go on, in its merry way. And while tragedy is concerned with the way we handle the problems of good and evil in the world, comedy deals with the lighter side of life by making us laugh at eccentrics, clowns, and absurdities. Through tragic catharsis, we rise above and gain control of the emotions of pity and fear, but through comic catharsis, we are purged of our worldly cares through a gush of pleasure in a joke or comic situation. The result is that we become carefree again, for comic pleasure momentarily reduces us to the state of carefree childhood and reconciles us to the world.

Above all, literature exists to perform two well-recognized functions: to teach and delight us, better expressed more succinctly by Horace: *dulce et utile* (to delight and teach), and *ridentem dicere verum* (I tell the truth, laughing, or in more idiomatic English: many a truth is told in jest). While literature teaches us, its entertainment side becomes the spoonful of sugar that makes the medicine go down. This double-barrelled function of literature aims at the development of the totality of the individual. And since man wants to aspire to be more than just himself, he runs to literature to complete himself, to make himself a WHOLE MAN. And man's aspirations to wholeness are seen concretely in his other ventures. Why does he get married? Isn't it because man does not wish to live in a world of men and women and not know the other half? So, man marries to complete himself. The same thing happens in the realm of literature. Man discovers that he cannot live in a world of emotions and experience, knowing only his own. He wants to partake, even if vicariously, of the emotions and experiences of others. In living for the most part life that is real and harsh, man cannot afford to deny himself experiences that catapult him into the world of romance and adventure. By partaking of these experiences through literature, man tries to enrich his experiences and make himself whole. So, he goes to the theatre, reads novels, and recites poetry written by others.

In especial, many people read great works of literature because literature gives the ordinary man who lacks the gifts of words to express adequately how he feels, the most eloquent words to express himself, and where he would ordinarily be dumb, the poet intervenes on his behalf and supplies the right but inspired words. In literature, also, we are all searching, as the adage says, for that truth that is big enough to live by, and great enough to die for. In the light of all we have said above about literature, we may disagree with Kant's dictum about the "purposive purposelessness" of art, for literature is committed to influencing a well-ordered, disciplined, fulfilled society-peopled by humanized individuals who are at the same time intellectually nourished by those petals of wisdom which only literature can offer. Wasn't it T. S. Eliot who advises us that in ceasing to care for literature "one ceases to care for those faculties and virtues demanded by literary practice, and this constitutes a special form of barbarism." This reminds one of Achebe's advice to a professor in Lagos who declared openly that he does not read anything beyond his narrow area of expertise. Achebe compared him to a four-cylinder engine operating on two plugs; any wayside mechanic will tell him that his engine is "missing fire."

Mr. Vice-Chancellor, Sir, my function today which I think I have performed to the best of my ability, it to offer literature to my colleagues and compatriots, those who wonder where I get the endless jokes I regale them with, so they can see and appreciate its refining propensities, its humanizing predilections, its intellectually nourishing content, for literature is a mighty agent of mind-enlargement, of intellectual liberation.

We are all aware that while the scientist deals with facts, the literary artist deals with man's capacity for wonder and delight. And pursuit of the delights revealed in literature means pursuit of refined tastes. And the ability to acquire refined tastes is born out of the appreciation of all the beauties hidden in literature: the appreciation of a well-turned phrase, the delight in the perfect choice of a word, in the sheer lyricism of poetry, in the beauty of total effect. To cultivate these beauties will ultimately lead to a life so harmoniously and completely developed and lived that we could proudly say of ourselves what Matthew Arnold said of Sophocles:

He saw life steadily And he saw it whole.

Finally let me paraphrase Dickens and say of myself that literature has done me good, and still does me good, and will

continue to do me good, and I say: GOD BLESS
LITERATURE!
   Ave Atque Vale

2

Literature, the Arts, and Cultural Development

Here we focus on the part literature and the arts have played in the landscape of national and cultural development in this country. The contours of that landscape will reveal the positive and often the unifying role literature and the arts, especially history and other subjects studied under the arts have played in the cultural and national development of Nigeria, and in the international and diplomatic recognition of Nigeria as a culturally advanced country in the community of nations. Since emphasis is on literature, there may be little room to smuggle in, the elevating and equally unifying role the visual and fine arts have equally played in the elevation of Nigeria in the eyes of the world. The Festac mask is almost a national emblem. Nigerian artefacts purloined by colonial powers still adorn British and other European museums. And we remember the heady days when the Queen of England as a young woman sat for several hours at a time, for several days, for Professor Ben Enwonwu. The above, by way of a preamble.

Let me begin by calling attention to Matthew Arnold's enlightening essay: "On the Modern Element in Literature". According to Arnold, the ideal modern epoch is attained when "a significant, a highly developed, a culminating epoch" exists, side by side with a "comprehensive, a commensurate, an adequate literature".[1]

I cite the above to draw attention to an envisaged culturally developed society — a society in which as Arnold asserts, there exists "the simultaneous appearance of a great epoch and a great literature." Such a society whether it is found in fifth century Athens or today, we must agree, should be regarded as artistically, historically, and culturally developed.

Now, if we must discuss a culturally developed and modern society, the onus is on us to understand by oblique references what culture consists in, and the implications of its opposite, anarchy. In "Sweetness and Light" Arnold quoting Montesquieu, asserts that culture exists "to render an intelligent being yet more intelligent" in order to make "reason and the will of God prevail."[2] But the man of culture he posits, is opposed by the philistine — the philistine being "people who believe most that our greatness and welfare are proved by our being very rich, and who give their lives ad thoughts to becoming rich."[3] The philistines are people with plebeian ambitions; people whose vulgar tastes pose a danger to culture, because "culture tends always with the men of a system, of discipline, of a school."[4]

When culture as just described is restricted only to the elite or confined to even a more restricted cabal among the elite — in a society mainly vulgarized by a majority of the vulgar rich, of vulgar philistines with plebeian tastes and propensities, the society is not only endangered but

---

[1] Matthew Arnold. "On the Modern Element in Literature," in *Victorian Poetry and Poetics,* (ed), Walter E. Houghton and Albert Stange (Boston: Houghton) Mifflin Co., 1968), p. 497ff.

[2] Matthew Arnold, "Sweetness and Light" in *Criticism:* The *Major Texts* (ed), Walter Jackson Bate (New York: Harcourt Brace and World, Inc., 1952), p. 467.

[3] Ibid, p.470.

[4] Ibid, p.471.

traumatized. Culture looks beyond vulgar wealth, beyond the febrile pursuit of the false symbols of life, beyond the rude display of meretricious and garish symbols of affluence, beyond ill-bred, foul-mouthed bragging about earthly possessions.

Culture, furthermore, takes root in a society when a way of life, when patterns of acquired behaviour, when routine acts of daily life are stanched into habit. Culture, in the individual and society, flows from the professor of belles-lettres, for example, to the man in the street so that a distinct pattern of civilized existence can be discerned as peculiar to a people. A culturally developed society such as we have in mind, would be as far away from anarchy as the saint is from the sinner, for anarchy thrives on lawlessness, approaching nihilism when a group, a cabal decides that the state such as we know it should be abolished and replaced by free association of groups, or when the more articulate among this cabal preach that all forms of government are incompatible with their own concept of individual liberty.

The Nigerian society at present, although swimming in its own ocean of anomie, may have just escaped being anarchic. But then, indiscipline, bribery, corruption, embezzlement of money from the public till, are rampant among us. And indiscipline is the junior brother to anarchy. Chinua Achebe in *The Trouble with Nigeria* describes indiscipline as "a failure or refusal to submit one's desires and actions to the restraints of orderly social conduct, in recognition of the rights and desires of others."[5] Where did we go wrong? Achebe had worried more about indiscipline among the ruling elite than among the populace because

---

[5] Chinua Achebe, *The Trouble with Nigeria* (Enugu: Fourth Dimension Publishers, 1983), p. 27

the indiscipline of the ordinary citizen, regrettable as it may be, does not pose a fatal threat to society because it can be generally contained by his fellows or, at worst, by a couple of policemen. But the indiscipline of a leader is a different matter altogether. First, he has no fellows to restrain him, and the policemen who might have done it are all in his employ. Second, power, by giving him immunity from common censure, makes the leader the envy of the powerless who will turn him into a role model and imitate his actions of indiscipline.[6]

Those of us in Nigeria who are old enough to remember, would easily recall the early 1950s and 1960s or the period before the civil war as an epoch of discipline, of day dreaming, of reaching out for the unattainable. It was the kind of epoch in our lives that Matthew Arnold would refer to as one of "Sweetness and Light" when there was a mighty surge to acquire knowledge rather than material wealth, when (to quote Arnold again) "the whole of society was in the fullest measure permeated by thought, sensible to beauty, intelligent and alive."[7] In the 1950s we were under the *Pax Britannica,* until the Civil War and the post-war oil boom dealt the death blow to things of the spirit and we found ourselves floundering in the swamps of the desires of the flesh.

Why are the 1950s and the early 1960s such a beautiful niche in our history, such an .oasis in our desert-journey to nationhood? It was an era when we found ourselves in-between two worlds-the world of regimentation by the British and the world of newly acquired independence within which to test the stuff of which we were made. And it was an era of the arts rather than of science and technology.

---

[6] Ibid, p.32.

[7] In Bate, p. 472

What does all this add up to when we say that the epoch under discussion was one of the arts rather than of technology? We mean that because we were all inspired and motivated by the kind of knowledge which the British championed and promoted (the classics, history, philosophy, language, literature, religion) we fell irretrievably and irremediably under the spell of those disciplines and the order and discipline which they imposed. We imbibed into ourselves imperceptibly as we voraciously swallowed what the British dished out to us at the University College, Ibadan, and at other government secondary schools headed mainly by expatriates, the known fact that literature and the other arts are of value to the degree that they enable man and society to fulfil what is best in them.

Furthermore, in the 1950s and early 1960s we were, through the discipline of history, straining to prove to the sneering white historians, to the likes of Hugh Trevor-Roper of Oxford (who impudently had asserted that African history was merely "the unrewarding gyrations of barbarous tribes in picture square but in irrelevant corners of the globe") that we are a people with history that was not an extension of Europe, and that according to Osuntokun:

> Africa is not only the home of man, the continent where man became man, it is also the place of ancient civilizations like that of Egypt. The contribution of Africans to world Civilizations of Kush, Axum, Nok, Kanem of Borno, Ghana, Mali, Songhai and the relatively recent ones of Ife, Igbo-Ukwu, and Benin... have led scholars to identify the positive effect of African civilization on what was supposed to be the creation of western genius.[8]

---

[8] Jide Osuntokun, "The Relevance of the Humanities and the Contribution of Nigeria to Civilization through the Humanities" in *The Humanities and National Development in*

The epoch marked by the 1950s and 1960s saw the full flowering in Nigeria, of what has been identified as cultural nationalism or cultural reaffirmation which, according to Obiechina, was aimed at reasserting the "African personality", at regaining cultural initiative, at rehabilitating the African culture in order to give our people "a new vision of life, to rescue them from the trauma of cultural confusion in which they have been left as a result of European acculturation, to provide them with new values, new outlooks and new spiritual bearing with their base in the African culture and psychology."[9]

This is the epoch when Achebe tells us in a lecture at Leeds University, 1965:

> Here then is an adequate revolution for me to espouse... to help my society regain belief in itself and put away the complexes of the years of denigration and self-abasement. I for one would not be excused. I would be quite satisfied if my novels (especially the ones I set in the past) did no more than teach my readers that their past...with all its imperfections... was not one long night of savagery from which the first Europeans acting on God's behalf delivered them.[10]

Achebe, of course, was not speaking in a historical vacuum. Nigerians were the inheritors of a literary movement that swept the Caribbean and the Francophone world in the 1930s and 1940s ... the Negritude movement.

The Negritude movement as I had said elsewhere had a catalytic effect on African literature. It was the centre-piece

Nigeria, (ed) A. E. Erevbetine and Nina Mba (Lagos: Nelson Publishers Ltd..., 1991), p. 59.

[9] Emmanuel Obiechina, "Cultural Nationalism in Modern African Creative Writing," *African Literature Today* (Vol. 1, No. 1, 1968), p. 32.

[10] Chinua Achebe, "The Novelist as Teacher" *in Morning Yet on Creation Day* (London: Heinemann, 1975), pp. 44 — 45.

of Africa's literary nationalism in the wake of political independence for all black peoples. To regain cultural initiative, to imbue political independence with national and cultural pride, to embark on the path of psychic reconstruction, were what energized the literary movement known as Negritude. Negritude, what Jean Paul Sartre calls "an antiracist racism" was embarked upon by writers of African descent as a form of literary therapy for the common welfare of all peoples of African descent to recover their essential selfhood bashed and mutilated by white arrogance through the colonial intrusion.[11]

We have dwelt on Achebe and the Negritude movement to point to the function of literature, as a branch of the arts, in the cultural development of our people. We have also touched on history as an aid in this journey to heal our wounded psyche, in restoring a sense of dignity and pride to a people denigrated as irrelevant in the march of civilization. Here also, we recall our dramatists — Rotimi, in *Kurunmi* and *Ovanranwen Nogbaisi*. Soyinka in *Death and the King's Horseman,* Osofisan in *Morountodun* all have reflected our past through projection and criticism of our national heroes by highlighting the strengths and weaknesses in the characters of our past from whom we learn the appropriate lessons in order to steer our ship of state to a better course. And through translations into various European and Asian languages, our literatures have gone international and have helped us carve out a definite niche in world culture. Our folklore, our manner of dress, our customs — all have permeated world culture through the collective endeavours of our artists.

In the light of the above, it becomes clear that Nigeria

---

[11] See Charles E. Nnolim "Literature and the Common Welfare" Inaugural Lecture, University of Port Harcourt (1988), pp. 15 — 16.

has definitely benefited, has definitely developed, has definitely become a more modern, a more stable society through the collective endeavours of our artists, through the collective contributions made in the realm of the arts. We cannot say this about our endeavours in the realm of the arts. We cannot say this about our endeavours in the realm of science and technology on which the Federal Government has pitched her tent, if we just cast a glance in the region of her lopsided J.A.M.B admission policy in favour of science and technology. Need we then be reminded that the arts make for order, for discipline, for refinement, for unity?

If, as we all agree, language is the bedrock of civilization and culture and is fundamental to the existence of human societies, we would appreciate the more its importance in Nigeria which is a country still striving after legitimacy as a nation. By an accident of history, English men and the English language may have made the existence of Nigeria as a geographical entity possible. English may be the official language of Nigeria and most of our internationally recognized writers write in English. But for our own cultural and national development, must we remain condemned in the use of that language which reminds us of our bondage to the imperial legacy of colonialism? To assume a language, it is agreed, is to assume a world view, to assume the cultural view of the owners of that language.

In our literature written in English, we recognize the gymnastic volleyball our writers have played with that language. According to Achebe, English in the hands of our writers has surrendered itself to all kinds of use; it has been bent, proverbialized, pidginized, domesticated, even vernacularised. But it is still the English language. If we can communicate easily in it with Ghanaians and Camerounians, where then does it acquire this divine afflatus to weld us together as a nation, as different from mere geographical entity? Granted, we can do little to dismiss the use of the English language in the immediate future, but knowing the importance of language in nation-building, must the Nigerian nation surrender itself to an *eternal* bondage to the English language?

These questions are necessary in the light of the Nigerian Government's language policy. True, use of the mother-tongue is encouraged in the early years of primary school. But this piece-meal approach to the language question will never build a strong, virile, patriotic, united Nigerian citizenry. Nigeria should make it *compulsory* for every Nigerian child to pass at the school certificate level, his mother-tongue and at least one other major language in Nigeria, and this would influence posting during the Youth Corps to consolidate the language learned in school, in the manner in which students of foreign languages spend a year abroad to consolidate knowledge of the language learnt by rote in school. In effect, a young Nigerian, if this suggestion is adopted, can influence his posting during his service year by the language he studied in school. An Ijaw should study either Hausa or Yoruba; a Hausa, either Igbo or Yoruba, *et cetera*. The present haphazard language policy does not have the building of one nation in mind.

And if we have not given up the idea of developing an indigenous technology (not a transferred one) we should pay urgent and insistent attention to the development of *indigenous* languages. A young Japanese student revealed recently that in looking over undergraduate notes taken by his ancestors in Japanese universities since the 1850s, he noted that his grandfather took all his notes in English, his father half in English and half in Japanese, and his own notes are completely in Japanese. And Japan, today, has a very strong indigenous technology — a technological base that is now the envy of Europe and America.

How does this affect us in Nigeria? Well, Nigeria wants a "transfer" rather than a development of indigenous technology by re-enforcing rather than discouraging the study of English at every stage of a youth's development. Secondly, the study of our indigenous language has suffered benign neglect through inadequate funding, lack of sponsorship of indigenous language newspapers and publications of books in the vernacular. One has no choice but urge urgent government attention to the development of languages and literatures in the mother-tongue and make compulsory the study and passing of a major second Nigerian language by all Nigerian youths at the School Certificate level, because knowledge and development of the mother-tongue is a major vehicle of acculturation and will help advance the cause of national unity and cultural identity. Furthermore, as Nnabuenyi Ugonna urges:

> Our technological revolution will continue to elude us so long as we fail to indigenize our technological language.

Because

> It is needful to stress here that in the African context, to make the scientific process fully understandable entails the imparting of science literacy in the indigenous language understood by the vast majority of people. Foreign technological language is so esoteric to a vast majority of the people that the hope of achieving an appreciable level of scientific literacy in it, is merely day-dreaming.[12]

This chapter has argued that Nigeria's arts and literatures have contributed immensely to her cultural and

---

[12] Nnabuenyi Ugonna, "Language and African Technological Development", in *The Humanities and National Development in Nigeria* pp. 167, 170.

national development. Nigerian writers have won her international fame and have placed Nigeria firmly on the literary map of the world. Her dramatists have helped to re-establish the African personality through cultural reaffirmation. Her historians have corrected the distortions about Africa's place in world history denied us by Europeans, and, as we have just stated above, we only now need a clear language policy in our educational endeavours to weld this country together into a nation that is more untied and more unified.

Why then the present anomie, the philistinism of the present post-civil war epoch, the vulgarism of the drug-assisted, get-rich-quick braggart, the pen-robber, contract inflation expert baron in our civil service and parastatals? Nigeria is in anomie because the moral force, the discipline, the order, the refinement which the era of the arts imposed before the civil war, are gone. Wasn't it T. S. Eliot who advised us that in ceasing to care for the arts and literature, "one ceases to care for those faculties and virtues demanded by literary practice, and this constitutes a special form of barbarism."

When government suddenly discovered science and technology as an alternative to the arts and the humanities, it forgot in the process that the arts and the humanities are the nurturers of science and technology, that according to Abimbola, "appropriate technology is a direct product of the values and norms of that particular society as nurtured in its humanities."[13]

Abimbola continues:

Rather than see the sciences as an absolute alternative to the

---

[13] Wande Abimbola, "The Humanities and National Consciousness", in *The Humanities and National Development in Nigeria*, p. 5.

humanities, we must understand the essential complementarity of both. Technology is a product of a people's culture as enunciated in the humanities. Like the female, the humanities conceive and give birth to the male child called technology. It is the mother's duty to nurture the child to maturity... science and technology must be seen as children of the humanities. A people who have no culture of their own cannot have a technology of their own...To develop our nation, therefore, the very first consideration is our culture, our values, and the enrichment of our thought process. It is only in a well organised society in which there is order, discipline, peace, respect for fellow human beings and political stability that you can talk of technological progress and economic growth.[14]

Now we must end this section of our discourse by refocusing this study on the liberating powers of literature. Although Matthew Arnold had asserted that poetry will save us, few societies have actually been saved or liberated by literature, although literary artists keep trying, at least to intellectually liberate their societies through their works.

II

As we now focus more closely on literature, the main emphasis of this study, we wish to draw attention to the unique role literature has played in our national life, on our cultural development; of the opportunities it offers and continues to offer Nigerians and the world to listen to its quiet voice and gain by its admonition. It is through literature, through poetry that Walter Malone, in a famous poem entitled "opportunity" urges us to disregard the self defeating adage that "opportunity occurs but once". He urges us in the poem to take courage because opportunity

---

[14] Ibid, pp. 5-6.

does, in fact, present itself again and again in our lives. The poem reads:

> They do me wrong who say I come no more
> When once I come and fail to find you in
> For everyday I stand outside your door
> And bid you wake and rise to fight and win.
>
> Wail not for precious chances passed away
> Weep not for golden ages on the wane
> Each night I burn the records of the day
> At sunrise every soul is born again.
>
> I cannot do it will never accomplish anything
> I'll try has done wonders.

Our own Wole Soyinka had declared in an entry in *World Authors*

> I believe implicitly that any work of art which opens out the horizons of the human mind and intellect, is by its very nature a force for change, a medium for change.[15]

With these two challenging dicta in mind, let us concentrate on what our Nigerian writers have done through literature to contribute their quota in the area of our culture and national development. We begin with their efforts to reconstruct our image, indeed Africa's image distorted and bruised by colonial intrusion, especially by white writers who saw in our humanity, climate, and landscape a savage people without history and humanity; saw in our climate an impenetrable jungle teeming with wild animals; and saw in our culture and traditions a senselessness that made an

---

[15] Bernth Lindfors, *In Person: Achebe, Awoonor,* and *Soyinka* Seattle: 1975), p. 135.

entire continent irrelevant in world history. Our writers have, through their works, risen to the challenge of giving valency to our traditions and culture by demonstrating through their works the logic in our traditional legal systems, the soundness in our healing ways, the meaning in our rituals, and the beauty in our art. This is what Emmanuel Obiechina calls "cultural nationalism" which aims at "rehabilitating the autochthonous culture".

Our writers, as we shall soon see, are socially committed. Their social commitment consists mainly in this: writing works that focus on what Nigerians have made of themselves since independence, attacking the corruption, the failure of leadership, the kleptomania by people in positions of power, plus the usurpation and abuse of power by the military elite. Our writers have used the power of literatures as a moral corrective, for literature exists in the main as a corrective to human folly, as a humanizing agent, and as the uplifter of our souls through its affective powers. As a well-recognized discipline in the humanities as we have hinted earlier, literature appeals to our sense of order, restraint, and discipline, imparting in its wake a sense of decorum and proportion.

Our writers are convinced that education in the humane letters is to be trusted to uplift our souls, to refine our behaviour, to move us away from the path of vulgarity, because a man educated in the humane letters is more likely to be a man of ethics, of lofty morals, and a man of refinement (although we don't hear of that word "refine" in Nigeria nowadays except in reference to petroleum products!) Our literary artists believe strongly with T. S. Eliot (in "Religion and Literature") that serious literature addresses itself to definite ethical and theological issues because "the greatness of literature cannot be determined solely by literary standards" since "literature must be backed by great ethical and religious support, for great works of literature have been and probably always will be judged by some moral standards"

It becomes evident that our literary artists are interested in the moral values of literature, as each saw his job through literature as that of reconstruction, of rehabilitation, or imparting moral values through literature.

In *A Man of the People* Achebe indicts several ills in post-independence Nigeria, especially those ills connected with the political life of our people: election malpractices, especially stuffing or breast-feeding the ballot box, use of thugs and political violence, and rigging to influence election results. He further attacks the ostentatious life-style of ministers, abuse of power after looting the nation's treasury, intolerance of opinions of those in opposing political camps, and blatant acts of bribery ad corruption by those entrusted to preserve the country's hard-won independence.

The hard lessons Achebe wants Nigerians to learn from *A Man of the People* (lessons that have unfortunately fallen on the nation's politically deaf ears) are that nemesis overtakes both the populace and the rulers who abuse the political system, even though they know the rules of the game, and that as long as the intellectuals leave the government of the country to illiterates who make a mockery of democracy, there will never be salvation for Nigeria, and by extension for Africa. As some critics have tried to point out, the two protagonists — Chief Nanga (Honourable, Chief, Dr, MA, MP), who is illiterate but who wields power and carries the people whom he cheats along with him (although devoid of any worthwhile political ideology), and Mr. Odili (who is enlightened and has some worthwhile ideas but has no political following) are like the two proverbial knives in the house of a widow: the one that is sharp has no handle, and the one that has a handle is not sharp. Nigeria, therefore, can only attain salvation when the dirty game of politics attracts more honest elite who have worthy political ideology. In the absence of this, only God will save us all: the suggested *deus ex machina* at the end, through military intervention.

Soyinka in *The Interpreters* and *Season of Anomy* is another writer who is concerned with moral issues in the Nigerian society. These two works, set also in post-independence Nigeria expose corruption and crime in the Nigerian body politic and a kind of conspiracy of silence among the elite (who act as the 'interpreters') who are ineffectually fiddling in bars and party halls while their country is burning. Effete intellectuals talk of "moral turpitude", while they live very immoral lives and are depicted in hilarious scenes that are not 'funny' at all: what with their endless frivolities, cheap gossip, endless drinking orgies — all showing wasted talent adrift in the moral wreckage of the country, while the corrupt chairman of the council and members of the Board of Interview are busy frustrating innovative engineers like Sekoni. In *Season of Anomy*, Soyinka presses his point further.

The term "anomy" was first coined by the French sociologist, Emile Durkheim, to refer to the absence of conditions necessary for man to fulfil himself and to attain happiness in his society. These conditions are that conduct should be governed by norms, that those norms should form an integrated and non-conflicting system, and that limits should be set to the pleasures attainable in life. Any state where there are unclear, conflicting or unintegrated norms, in which the individual has no morally significant relations with others or in which there were no limits set to the attainment of pleasure, is in a state of anomy.[16] Both the

---

[16] Emmanuel Obiechina, "The Writer and the His Commitment in Contemporary Nigerian

individual and the society in a state of anomy have lost their moral bearings, lost their moral roots, and are cast adrift in a situation where neither the society nor the individual has any standards to uphold and is thoroughly vulgarized. A state of anomy thus subsumes conflicts between value systems resulting in stress and anxieties, plus the deterioration of values and standards and the disintegration of values at large.

But Soyinka's Aiyero, exploited and brutalized by the profit-hungry cartel, reflects in-depth the dangerous and harassed path which the Nigerian society currently treads. The activities of the cartel and the blood-letting unleashed on fellow citizens of the Cross River, led by Zaki Amuri, are re-enactments of events in Nigeria before the civil war. Wanton destruction of life and property are moral issues; unfair election practices, bribery and corruption, are moral issues dwelt on by our novelists. The Nigerian writer, therefore, is not a helpless onlooker but a courageous fighter against the moral decadence in our society. Achebe and Soyinka tackle these problems by making satiric thrusts at the ills of our society.

Okara in *The Voice* tells a not-so-gory tale, but the subtlety of his artistic vision is very penetrating. The activities of Chief Izongo, who buys people's consciences and intimidates them into compliance and acquiescence, are etched in a very vivid light. Then, a moral voice, quiet and insistent is introduced: that of Okolo ("the voice"). This voice makes Chief Izongo and his cabal rather uncomfortable, and all of them collude to destroy Okolo. Okolo's obsessive quest, asking people if they have got 'it' threatens the immoral and timid elements of the society, for he is asking them if they were satisfied with the way they were governed, with the quality of their lives, and whether they have allowed Chief Izongo "to buy the insides of all the people". And he goes further to ask Abadi, who has got his MA and PhD but not `it', why this is so. Okolo, that voice in the wilderness, crying for the moral regeneration of his society, accuses the rulers and politicians of having accepted "the shadow-devouring trinity of gold, iron, concrete," reminding them that the worst enemies of the society are those who say like the messenger: "As for me... if the world turns this way, I take it. Any way the world turns. I take it with my hands. I like sleep... so I do not think," and like the elder who thinks nothing can be done when he says: "If they do anything I agree, since they do not take yam out of my mouth." All these people Okolo condemns as "think-nothing people" who are "like logs in the river" and "float and go whither the current commands." These, of course, are the people of Sologa who bundled Okolo and Tuere and exiled them in a floating canoe with their limbs tied up, so that they inevitably drowned in a whirlpool.

What Okara tells us in *The Voice* is that the onus of moral regeneration in our society lies with the intellectuals. Nietzsche said "society needs an elite that will set a pattern and curb the thoughtlessness of the masses." This Okolo tried to do and lost his life. This Odili of *A Man of the People* tried to do but had not the power base to accomplish. To this the "interpreters" of Soyinka's novel woefully failed to address themselves. All the authors discussed so far have one common premise: that the burden of ridding our society of bribery, corruption, and immorality lies with the intellectuals.

The Nigerian writer, it is clear, sees himself as an individual with definite responsibilities. As Emmanuel Obiechina argues, the Nigerian writer:

Should have a special allegiance to the down trodden in the Nigerian society, to the socially handicapped, to the women, the children, the unemployed, the sick; all those who are not able to fight their own battles. The writer should put on his armour and charge into battle in defence of the defenceless. It is my view that the writer in Nigeria of today has to take his position against the oppression of the people, all forms of brutalities, and of unwarranted violence against the masses.[17]

As if in support of the above, the younger more revolutionary minded writers in our country, those in the camp of Omotoso, Sowande, Osofisan, Odia Ofeimun, and Festus Iyayi, some of them clearly Marxist in ideology, ally with the masses and urge a revolution that would cleanse society of its present ills. Envisaging a classless society, Omotoso *(in The Edifice, The Combat, Sacrifice),* Femi Osofisan (in *Kolera Kolej),* Sowande (in *Our Man the President),* and Iyayi (in *Violence)* — this younger group of writers see literature as an instrument of liberation, urging the masses to rise up and overthrow the oppressive system. In Iyayi's *Heroes,* the protagonist urges a third army to rise up and liberate the cheated and betrayed masses. These younger writers are not really alone. The older Soyinka had urged us in *A Shuttle in the Crypt:*

Take justice
In your hands who can
Or dare, insensate sword
Of power...
Orphans of the World
Ignite! Draw
Your fuel of pain from earth's sated core.

---

[17] *A New Dictionary of Sociology,* (ed) G. Duncan Mitchel (London: Routledge & Kegan, 1979), p. 7.

In *Season of Anomy,* Soyinka unabashedly insists on a bloody revolution to remove the oppressive regime. Demakin the Dentist urges his men:

> Extract the carious tooth quickly... But we must also set up a pattern of killing the more difficult ones. Select the real kingpins and eliminate them. It is simple, you have to hit the snake on the head to render it harmless...The harmattan...is the right season for insurrections. Fires burn faster, the winds fly drier, a people's anger spirals swifter in the dust of those miniature devil-winds building up into the cyclone that must sweep off their oppressors.[18]

But Achebe, always on the side of caution, advises reform rather than revolution, the consequences fa which might be cataclysmic. In *Anthills of the Savannah* he tells us:

> Experience and intelligence warn us that man's progress in freedom will be piecemeal, slow and undramatic. Revolution may be necessary for taking a society out of an intractable „stretch of quagmire, but it does not confer freedom, and may indeed hinder it... Reform may be a dirty word then but it begins to look more and more like the most promising route to success in the real world.[19]

In the light of the above, will literature save Nigeria? Will Matthew Arnold's dictum that "poetry will save us" be finally realized in Nigeria?
Will Amin Baraka's

> Assassin poems, poems that shoot guns

---

[18] Wole Soyinka, *Season of Anomy.* (London: Thomas Nelson and Sons, 1980), pp. 92, 111.

[19] Chinua Achebe, *Anthills of the Savannah,* (Ibadan: Heinemann, 1988) p. 99.

Poems that wrestle cops into alleys
And take their weapons, leaving them dead,

save a country like Nigeria? Or should we succumb to the despair and apparent helplessness sketched in Don Lee's dictum:

I ain't seen no poems stop a .38
I ain't seen no stanzas break
A honkie's head
I ain't seen no metaphors stop a tank.

The level-headed thing to do is to steer the middle course. No, we cannot point to a society "saved" by literature. And yes, literature has been influential in changing societies and individuals. In fact, literature has once helped save a soul. Emile Zola's "J' Accuse" (1898) inspired by the Dreyfus Affair led to the release of Captain Dreyfus; and Andre Gide's work, *Voyage au Congo* led in modern history to the termination of King Leopold's hold on that nation, by exposing the atrocities perpetrated by Belgians against the Congolese people.

So, as we turn our attention briefly from the writers to their products, we may ask: what has literature done for Nigeria, for instance? Why does it deserve a place in the scheme of things, in our educational system? Well, we may ask: has it ever occurred to any one of us that while technology could be "transferred" literature and the arts belong uniquely to a people. Literature like tradition and culture, is autochthonous; and if we allow literature and the arts to die through neglect, our very humanity, our identity as a people will not only be under threat but it will disappear, and our very identity in world culture will face complete effacement.

Nigeria, of course, need no longer entertain any such

fears. We are not only the pathfinders in African literatures, we are the undisputed leaders in that field. Our literatures have indeed fostered national consciousness, patriotism and nationalism. Every Nigerian holds his head high anywhere in the world because Achebe, Okara, Soyinka, Ola Rotimi, Niyi Osundare, Festus Iyayi, Ken Saro-Wiwa and Ben Okri are indigenes of this great country of literary giants. Nigeria's most valued export commodity is not petroleum products but her literatures which have won every imaginable international prize including the Nobel Prize. Achebe's works alone, by the latest count, have been translated into fifty different languages outside Africa. Through her literatures as mentioned above, Nigeria exports her culture and tradition to other parts of the world and, through these literary works, exposes to the world the very foundations of her national consciousness.

At the level of society, the aesthetic experience fosters mutual sympathy and understanding which will normally help, on a larger scale, to draw men together, to draw our country together, since all shared experience helps to bring people together in friendship and national respect., for any group of people who share the same aesthetic experience have a bond between them, and feel united under a common identity. So, Nigerian literatures unite Nigerians more than politics or science or religion.

Nigeria today stands tall before the international community because of the collective endeavours of her writers. While our politics and the shenanigans of our business deals most often sell Nigeria's private shames in the international scandal market, it is through the collective endeavours of Nigerian writers that Nigeria stands redeemed and enhanced in the eyes of the world, since the onus of moral regeneration in our society has always lain with our writers, as if in response to Nietzsche's call that "society needs an elite that will set a pattern and curb the thoughtlessness of the masses."

Nigerian writers have a accomplished this by establishing what I refer to as the Nigerian tradition in literature — a tradition that has set a pattern for the entire continent. It is that tradition which makes use of and expresses allegiance to our folk culture by creatively making use of our proverbs, local myths, folk tales, *et cetera,* in giving expression to our national culture by stridently stressing what is indigenous to Nigeria. Tutuola, Achebe, Soyinka, Elechi Amadi, Okigbo, Ola Rotimi, and many others were all concerned with cultural assertion and were pioneers in what we have come to regard as cultural nationalism in Nigerian literature: in their stressing the innate dignity of the Nigerian, in their concern with the rehabilitation of the image of the black man in general, and the Nigerian man and woman in particular: that image damaged and distorted by white writers. They have all established this tradition mainly through myth-making, through the mythopoeia of group identity and group experience, thereby transmitting culture, pursuing an ideology of cultural renaissance, emphasizing our communal and collective philosophy, stressing the success stories or failures of communities rather than the fortunes or misfortunes of the individual, calling attention to a rural rather than an industrial or technological way of life that has led to a fulfilled way of existence. They have done this by bending, twisting and proverbializing the English language or revealing the innate wealth of our vernacular languages.

And one should not leave the Nigerian female writer out of this discourse. Again it is the Nigerian female writer, Flora Nwapa, who set the pace both for Nigeria and the entire continent as the trail blazer in modern African female fiction writing and is therefore historically important. She saw it as her duty to redeem and correct the disparaged and debased image of the Nigerian woman as the women saw it depicted by male writers like Achebe and Cyprian Ekwensi — women created helpless, dependent, brutalized, disparaged, living either as prostitutes, concubines or "kept women", destined in the words of Chikwenye Ogunyemi "to carry *foofoo* and soup to men discussing important matters". Nwapa set the pace for the feminist trend in Nigerian literature, quickly joined by Buchi Emecheta, Zulu Sofola, Zaynab Alkali, Ifeoma Okoye, and a host of others by preaching the dignity and economic independence of Nigerian women in captivating titles like *Women Are Different* (Nwapa) and *Double Yoke* (Emecheta).

Far from being parasites, far from being dependent on their men, the feminist Nigerian woman is highlighted as dignified in comportment, economically independent, highly industrious and possessing superior and higher moral values than their male counterparts. Through their writings, the image of the Nigerian woman as equal in all respects with her male counterpart is now firmly established.

In sum, the Nigerian writer for love of his country has taken great risks to ensure that we live in a free and democratic society where no one is oppressed. The ultimate end toward which the writer tends is utopia, for the writer is essentially a dreamer envisaging a heaven on earth, freedom from racial, colonial and neo-colonial abuse, in short, a golden era of opportunities. Writers are finally the interpreters of our culture, the enemy of sinister forces in society, the conserver of our values, the terror of bad governments.

If, then, Nigeria realizes as it should that it is not through science but through our literatures and literary artists that she has gained the greatest international attention and fame, it would not be too much to ask the

Federal Government and we do ask her now to:

a) completely fund the Annual Symposium and the publications of the Nigerian Academy of Letters;

b) build the Nigerian Academy of Letters a permanent secretariat with a well-funded, well built-up and well maintained writers and artists village attached to it; where symposium, workshops, seminars are held;

c) establish and fund a post, similar to that of the poet-laureate in England, to be held by one outstanding writer for a life time, as a way of encouraging and honouring our outstanding and talented writers; or at least fund an annual prize for one outstanding writer to be designated as "Writer of the Year";

d) fund the post of writer-in-residence or artist-in-residence for our most eminent writers and artists in designated universities, in order to provide maximum exposure of our writers and artists to aspiring students;

e) encourage through adequate funding, the rehabilitation, teaching and propagation of our vernacular literatures and languages in both primary and secondary schools for purposes of validating our myths, folklore and oral culture which are the bedrock of all our written literatures?

The Federal Government is urged to do the above as a token of her recognition and appreciation of the salutary presence of artists and creative writers in her midst as shapers of public opinion, as vendors of truth, and as the most patriotic members in her polity.

Finally, I am deeply thankful to the Nigerian Academy

of Letters, and to her Secretary, Professor Segun Odunuga, for inviting me to deliver this year's lecture. And to this wonderful audience, quite patient and sympathetic, I cede to you my admiration. I doff my hat.

And for the Nigerian Academy of Letters, may the prestige of Plato's Academy attend all your endeavours. May the humanism of the Renaissance ventilate all your deliberations. May the spirit of scientific inquiry and the miraculous technological breakthroughs of the twentieth century energize all future activities.

3

The writer's responsibility and literature in national development

One's own self conquered is better than all other people conquered; not even a god could change into defeat the victory of a man who has vanquished himself.

- Buddha

Most readers think that the creative writer is there mainly to tell a story and entertain. This paper will try to demonstrate that far from merely telling an interesting story and entertaining, the creative writer wears more than one garb; he undertakes to be of definite use to his society and to humanity as a whole.

To begin with, man, according to Aristotle, is a political animal, and no one need be surprised that imaginative literature would naturally gravitate into the area of politics which normally deals with the day-to-day management of public affairs. The formalist may talk of "the poem per se," of beauty being its own excuse for being, of a poem (or novel for that matter) not existing to teach or even to please but to exist and be beautiful, but the discerning reader knows that art is propaganda where the writer is the persuasive purveyor of truth even if, in higher art, the end-result is an aesthetic experience.[1] In the main, though, most literary periods are influenced by political events which, some assert, have become the major determinant of norms in the periodization of literary history. Political events seem to be the sole determinant of literary history: periods like "Commonwealth" and "Restoration" are used for English Literature, "Colonial" and "Revolutionary" in American Literature; and "Pre-Independence" and "Post-Independence" periods in African Literature.

But beyond lending mere appellations to literary periods, politics enters literature through the latter's affective powers, through what we normally term, the pragmatic theory of art for, directed always toward the audience, the pragmatic theory looks at art as an end, since every writer wants to change the perceptions of his audience, to give that audience a new way of looking at an experience. In the affective or pragmatic theory of art, we use the adage:

> Some wish to change men's minds;
> Others wish to change the world men live in.

The political novel in Nigeria and West Africa seems to adhere to Frantz Fanon's "fighting phase" (third phase) of colonial and post colonial literature, when "the native... turns himself into an awakener of the people; hence comes a fighting literature, and a national literature."[2] Nigerian literature is, from its inception, an exercise in politically creative commitment. I define, therefore, in the broadest terms as political any literary endeavour in which the author's concerns with public themes and public welfare are

---

[1] Theodora Ezeigbo, "Functionality in Literature, Art and Propaganda", Savannah, Vol. 1, June (1989), p. 79.

[2] Frantz Fanon, *The Wretched of the Earth,* translated by Constance Farrington, (London, McGibbon & Kee, 1965, p. 179

predominant; especially any themes that extend beyond concerns of the individual self and embrace the collective destiny of nations or the masses. Politics enters literature at those times when the fate or destiny of peoples or classes are locked in the death-throes of survival, when continuity in a people's way of life is threatened; when alien forces by way of military forces or colonial invasion endanger a people's future or make that future uncertain; and, in our body politic, when the vultures of corruption descend to devour a people's cherished ethical religious or moral values.

In the light of the above, Nigerian literature was born in response to colonial invasion and its abuses which threatened our collective security as a people; it has since then been sustained by reaction to our collective disenchantment with political independence; and it will further thrive by protests to abuses inherent in the inequities engendered by the kind of society we have chosen to operate--inequities that have often erupted into open class or ethnic warfare. In the end, this study will posit that what unites our writers is utopia--their single-minded quest for a just and egalitarian society free from oppression and exploitation by both external and internal masters:

> Force and right are the governors of this world; Force till right
> is ready (Jourbert in *Pensees*)

The goal toward which our writers tend is that golden era when right will be ready, cushioned, of course, by economic abundance and the absence of want. Nigerian writers are therefore in quest of that epoch in our life-time or in not-so- distant a future when (now that we have achieved political independence) bribery and corruption will be wiped out from our body politic; for that time when intellectuals will take over political control which they have hitherto left in the hands of illiterate politicians and the military; for that time when politics is played here, as in Europe and the West, according to the rules of the game.

In Anglophone West Africa, the writer revealed in very bad light the subversion of post-Independence hopes and promises by those who were banked upon to redress the wrongs inflicted by the colonial masters. "Seek ye first the political kingdom" was the battle cry by Nkrumah who asked for the opportunity to be given Africans "to govern or misgovern themselves". Disenchantment ensued unfortunately when the "political kingdom" was achieved and the rulers including Nkrumah, set out on a path of misgoverning themselves. In novels by T.M. Aluko *(One Man, One Matchet);* Achebe (A *Man of the People);* Munonye (A *Wreath for the Maidens);* Armah *(The Beautyful Ones Are Not Yet Born)--all* made subtle and overt suggestions as they expressed their disenchantment with our failure to successfully operate a party-system democracy as they pointed out in disgust the circumambient presence of bribery and corruption in our body-politic; as they expressed the hope that political salvation might lie in the involvement of the intellectuals in party politics.

It should be re-stated that many creative artists write during periods dominated by intense political activity and major struggles, especially in times of war or major revolutions or struggles for independence; in times of great patriotic fervour; and from the desire to teach and speak for large masses of people. We may add that literature and politics are hardly separate and separable in the sense that political developments could determine the course of literature and in certain times, literary activities have been known to influence political developments. In France, for example, Emile Zola's *J'accuse* and Andre Gide's *Voyage au*

Congo were inspired by the Dreyfus episode and the Congo question respectively. They, in turn, helped to determine the outcome of these two issues: the one leading to the release of Captain Dreyfus, and the other leading to the termination of King Leopold's hold on the Congo.[3] In the United States of America, the civil war embarked upon by President Lincoln to emancipate the slaves was supposedly triggered off by Harriet Beecher Stowe's *Uncle Tom's Cabin,* so that when the author was introduced to Lincoln after the war he quipped: "Are you the little woman who started this war?"

The desire to speak for the masses, and to free them from political and economic strangulation has led to another brand of literature in West Africa championed by avowed socialist and Marxism-oriented writers. Their main aim is to achieve the Marxist utopia--equality of the classes--by imbuing the oppressed populace if possible, with enough revolutionary fervour to rise up and effect a social revolution. In Nigeria: we have Festus Iyayi *(Violence, The Contract);* Kole Omotoso *(The Edifice, The Combat)* Femi Osofisan *(Kolera Kolej):* Bode Sowande *(Our Man Mr. President);* Sonala Olumhense *(No Second Chance).* In the Ivory Coast and Senegal, Dadie's *(Climbie)* and Ousmane Sembene's *God's Bits of Wood and Le Docker Noir* carry forward the struggle of African trade unionists to effect, if possible, the dictatorship of the proletariat and achieve the political-cum-socialist utopia advocated by Karl Marx.

Although not noticed by many, Nigerian and West African female writers have embarked upon the writing of works with the lodestars of political implication. Their works are, in the main, radical in orientation and feminist in contemporary literary parlance, and the feminist posture

---

[3] Raymond Okafor, "Politics and Literature in the Ivory Coast", *Kiabara,* Vol. II (1979), p. 166.

they have assumed makes a strong political statement. Read Nwapa's *Efuru,* and you cannot miss the aggressive and fierce independence of the heroine; and read *Idu* and you find a debased man like Amarajeme who has no inner resources, who constantly borrows money from his wife and who, when his wife deserts him hanged himself with a rope from the thatched roof of his hut. Nwapa's rambunctious "daughter" Buchi Emecheta carries the feminist trend rather too far in *Second Class Citizen,* but the technique is the same adopted by Nwapa, especially in *One is Enough.* What these women and their followers elsewhere in West Africa (Aminata Sow Fall and Mariama Ba) do specifically is to fight sexism and male chauvinism in our literatures by debasing the image of the man and elevating that of the woman, and by creating women who are fiercely independent, who are capable of economic self-sufficiency, and who are "not anybody's appendage".

The aim is to present a "corrected" image of the female (normally debased, helpless, dependent, a prostitute, a concubine, in the hands of male writers). Mariama Ba in *So Long a Letter* carries on her own feminist, private warfare (supported by Aminata Sow Fall) against the practice of polygamy in Moslem West African countries. Polygamy, she urges, places educated women in a second class role, breaks hearts, breaks families, and sometimes places the hapless men she creates, in very untenable and debasing positions.

I have hinted earlier that literary works emerge also in times of war, and the Nigerian civil war gave rise to a large harvest of war novels each determined to make a strong political statement. I have in an earlier publication[4] adduced the following reasons why the ex-Biafrans wrote war novels:

---

[4] Charles E. Nnolim, "Trends in the Nigerian Novel". *Matatu,* Vol.2 (January, 1987), pp.7-22

1. Self-exculpation: to demonstrate that Biafrans had this ugly war imposed on victimized, blameless, oppressed Igbos by blood-thirsty and hate-filled Nigerians.

2. To put the historical records straight and record a memorable if traumatic experience in the political life of Nigeria and for the benefit of posterity.

3. For propaganda purposes: To score a diplomatic point by pointing out to the international community the real and hidden issues involved in the war and to prick the conscience of the allies on the "wrong" side of the conflict by subtle hints to them about the course of action they should have taken had they known the "facts".

4. To propagate the impression that while the shooting war was over, peace had not been won and that the struggle continues, especially the struggle for full reintegration into the mainstream of Nigerian life.

5. To recapture the Biafran manhood lost in the battle-field and substitute the power of the pen for the impotence of the Biafran soldiers armed with sticks and light weapons against the Nigerians' superior firepower, and in the process to highlight the pyrrhic nature of the Nigerian victory which was an overkill: the giant who jubilates for crushing a baby.

6. To depict the sufferings and the agonies, the dislocations and brutalities experienced by civilians during the conflict and to highlight the greed and corruption of officials in high places who have cashed in on the tribulation of the populace as opportunities for self-enrichment.

7. To demonstrate to outsiders the true state of affairs within Biafra by showing that all was not well within,

that the Biafran army was at war with itself and was at times experiencing a civil war within a civil war--the army against itself and the civilians against the armed forces, and that at certain points during the war, the ideals of that war, for Biafra, were subverted from within, leading to mass disenchantment.

8. On a higher artistic level, to re-order reality and experience made chaotic by the war situation.

Those interested in reading the Nigerian war novel will find the following authors and titles useful:

Victor Uzoma Nwankwo, *The Road to Udima*, 1969
John Munonye, *A Wreath for the Maidens*, 1973
I.N.O Aniebo, *The Anonymity of Sacrifice*, 1974
Flora Nwapa, *Never Again*, 1975
Eddie Iroh, *Forty-eight Guns for the General*, 1976, *Toads of War*, 1979, and *The Sirens in the Night*, 1982
Cyprian Ekwensi, *Survive the Peace*, 1976, and *Divided We Stand*, 1980
Ossie Enekwe, *Come Thunder*, 1984
Isidore Okpewho, *The Last Duty*, 1976
Andrew Ekwuru, *Songs of Steel*, 1979

The duty of the artist to influence change in his society is not without risks. One might recall the fate of artists and writers over the centuries. In mythology, King Minos of Crete imprisoned Daedalus and his son Icarus in the labyrinthine mazes the king had ordered the artificer Daedalus to construct for the Minotaur. The myth of the escape of Daedalus by fashioning wings for himself and his son (who flew too high and plummeted to earth for disobeying his father's instruction), has become the myth of the artist fashioning the mode of his own salvation. But note that the harassment of Daedalus and his son is the harassment which all artists face.

But that is myth. In history, the story of Socrates, that questioning gadfly who made uncomfortable even a democracy as established as the Greeks, must arrest our attention. Did they not arrest him, detain him, condemn him to death and give him hemlock to drink, on these charges:

> That Socrates is a criminal and a busybody, prying into things, under the earth and up in the heavens, and making the weaker argument the stronger, and teaching these things to others;
> That Socrates is a criminal who corrupts the young and does not believe in the gods whom the state believes in, but other new spiritual things instead.[5]

You will remember how Socrates, the one man the Delphic oracle pronounced "the master of them that know" quipped: "what a blessing it would be for young people if the whole nation of the Athenians makes them (the youth) fine gentlemen and I alone corrupt them," and then refused to escape from prison in a boat smuggled in by his friends for that purpose, because it would confirm his accusers in their false belief that he is a criminal who now has made himself a fugitive from justice. Such an escape he argued, would destroy the laws of Athens and render them nugatory. He, therefore, decided to stick by the truth, for truth, as he ingeniously argued, is a cleansing from vice, and wisdom commands him to obey the laws of the state and accept his punishment.

In our own days, we all remember how Aleksandr

---

[5] *The Great Dialogues of Plato* ed. Eric H. Warminton and Philip G. Rouse. New York: Mentor Books, (1956), pp.425, 430.

Solzhenitsyn, the 1970 Nobel Laureate, defied the KGB and published *The Gulag Archipelago* (1973), a documentary expose of the Soviet Secret Police, its prison camps, and its methods of terror and torture. The stir caused by this publication both in Russia and the West led to a dramatic development. After refusing to answer the summons to appear before government investigators ("before asking that citizens obey the law, learn to obey the law yourselves"), he told the government, Solzhenitsyn, who had spent eleven years in Russia's prison camps, was accused of high treason, stripped of his Soviet citizenship, had a decree read to him ordering his deportation without his family, and was hustled aboard an airliner and flown to West Germany. That was on February 12, 1974.

In apartheid South Africa, the scattering of her black writers abroad through banning orders is fresh in our memories. Dennis Brutus tells us how in 1965, he was imprisoned and tortured in Robben Island and "banned from publishing anything." In Kenya writing has proved also to be a risky enterprise. On December 31, 1977, Ngugi wa Thiong'o, the maverick Kenyan writer was arrested and detained in Kamiti Maximum Security Prison in Kiambu, Kenya, where he said: "I was kept behind stone walls and iron bars for a whole year." He had protested that "detention without trial is really a denial of the democratic rights of a Kenya national...I have never, even now, been told any specific reasons for my detention."[6] And in Nigeria, Wole Soyinka was detained from August 1967 to October 1969. He had declared in an entry in *World Authors:* "I have one abiding religion--human liberty" and he avowedly uses art to challenge unacceptable situations in society, having allegedly held up a radio station to forestall Chief Akintola's

---

[6] *The Weekly Review.* Nairobi: (January 5, 1979), p.30.

victory address in a rigged election, and having declared elsewhere:

> I believe implicitly that any work of art which opens out the horizons of the human mind, and intellect, is by its very nature, a force for change, a medium for change.[7]

In the light of the above, the serious creative writer must, therefore, ask himself why he writes. Is he with or against his society or is he a mere entertainer, or does he write for the betterment of his society? Is he a "safe" writer, a mere polite chronicler of events and suffering from that ashen paralysis which numbs action knowing that evil persists because good men say or do nothing? The serious writer must be committed and should not be an Abadi in Okara's *The Voice* who has got his MA and PhD but has not got "it". He should not be the elder in the same novel who thinks nothing can be done: "if they do anything, I agree since they do not take yam out of my mouth."

The Nigerian writer, for instance, as Emmanuel Obiechina argues:

> should have a special allegiance to the downtrodden in the Nigerian society, to the socially handicapped, to the women, the children, the unemployed, the sick; all those who are not able to fight their own battles. The writer should put on his armour and charge into battle in defence of the defenceless. It is my view that the writer in Nigeria of today has to take his position against the oppression of the people, all forms of brutalities, and of unwarranted violence against the masses.[8]

This should be applied to any other country. In the light

---

[7] *In Person: Achebe, Awoonor and Soyinka.* Seattle: Washington Institute of Comparative and Foreign Area Studies, University of Washington (1975), p.135.

[8] Emmanuel Obiechina, "The Writer and his Commitment in Contemporary Nigerian Society", *Okike,* Nos. 27/28, March (1988), p.4.

of the above, it is clear that the reader demands of our writers some measure of commitment, some degree of courage to challenge the status quo, to change our society long in anomie. The writer must definitely tell us where he stands. He must, in his works, confront the problem of good and evil in his society, differentiate them and take sides; and in taking sides, he must tell us and the masses of this country, where he stands. If he is not for us--the masses of this country--then, he cannot but be against us. He cannot, therefore, be a hypocrite--chasing with the hounds and at the same time running with the deer.

A majority of our writers, if not all, started on a patriotic note each was a writer with political radar. Each saw his job as that of reconstruction, of rehabilitation, of defence against the psychological wounds and denigration inflicted upon the people by the colonial invaders. Read Nnamdi Azikiwe and see his defence of Africa's dignity, of our place in world history denied us by European writers. Azikiwe tells us in *Renascent Africa* (Accra, 1937):

> Educate the renascent African to be a man. Tell him that he had made definite contribution to history. Educate him to appreciate the fact that iron was discovered by Africans, that the conception of God was initiated by Africans, that Africa ruled the world from 765 to 713 B.C., that while Europe slumbered during the "dark ages", a great civilization flourished on the banks of the Niger, extending from the salt mines of Therghazza in Morocco to lake Tchad. Narrate to him the lore of Ethiopia, of Ghana or Songhay. Let him relish with the world that, while Oxford and Cambridege were in their inchoate stages, the University of Sankore, in Timbuctoo, welcomed scholars and learned men from all over the Moslem world, as Sir Percy put it. (p.9)

The above was a partial rejoinder to the arrogance and

impudence of Hugh Trevor-Roper of Oxford who had asserted that African history was merely, "the unrewarding gyrations of barbarous tribes in picture square, but in irrelevant corners of the globe."

Mbonu Ojike, the boycott king of Nigeria, had also patriotically reacted against the false social theories propounded by Leo Africanus, Gobineau, and Levy-Bruhl. *My Africa* (New York: 1964), by Ojike was a defence of Africa's dignity, a rehabilitation of the African Personality. The European, he asserts,

> assumes that the African has neither laws nor political organizations; that the society is therefore chaotic, living in a miasma of tribal disorder...I wonder how much longer these fictions can blind the West (p.192).

With the above in mind, Achebe's dictum below has an accredited and noble ancestry:

> Here then is an adequate revolution for me to espouse- to help my society regain belief in itself and put away the complexes of the years of denigration and self-abasement.[9]

Africa's earlier writers, it will now be seen-these writers, whom critics refer to as Negritudinists, including Achebe, were concerned with reconstructing Africa's image distorted and bruised by colonial intrusion, especially by white writers who saw in Africa a savage people without humanity, saw in its climate an impenetrable and uninhabitable jungle teeming with wild animals, dispensing only illness and death to the white man; and saw in Africa's culture and traditions a senselessness that made an entire continent irrelevant in world history. These early pioneer writers have risen to the

---

[9] Chinua Achebe, "The Novelist as Teacher", In *Morning yet on Creation Day,* London: Heinemann, (1975), p.44

challenge of giving valency to our traditions and cultures by demonstrating through their works the logic in our traditional legal systems, the soundness in our healing ways, the meaning in our rituals, and the beauty in our art. This is what Obiechina calls "cultural nationalism" among African writers, which aims at "rehabilitating the autochthonous culture"; for the Nigerian writer, like his other African and black counterparts, must possess at all times, the highest measure of social consciousness. And, as Chinweizu and his group cogently put it:

> The function of the artist in Africa, in keeping with our traditions and needs, demands that the writer, as a public voice, assume a responsibility to reflect public concerns in his writing... because in Africa, we recognize commitment is mandatory of the artist.[10]

This social commitment wears many faces. Having chased away the colonial fox from without, the Nigerian writer, for instance, came home to admonish the barnyard hen within. This he did by writing pungent satirical works that focus on what Nigerians have made of themselves since Independence, attacking especially the corruption, the bribery, the failure of leadership, the kleptomania by people in positions of power, and the usurpation and abuse of power by the military elite.

While Achebe (in *A Man of the People)* and Aluko (in *One Man One Matchet)* merely held their protagonists up for ridicule, Soyinka, of this older vanguard, was not as patient or as subtle. He is for revolution, as he argues in *A Shuttle in the Crypt*:

---

[10] "Towards the Decolonization of African Literature", Okike, Vol. VII, June (1975), pp. 78-79

> Take justice
> In your hands who can
> Or dare, insensate sword
> Of power
> Outherods Herod and the law's outlawed
> ...Orphans of the world
> Ignite! Draw
> your fuel of pain from earth's sated core

In *Season of Anomy,* Soyinka unabashedly insists on a bloody revolution to remove an oppressive regime. Demakin the dentist urges his men:

> Extract that carious tooth quickly before it infects the others...
> But we must also set up a pattern of killing the more difficult
> ones. Select the real kingpins and eliminate them. It is simple,
> you have to hit the snake on the head to render it
> harmless...The harmattan...is the right season for insurrection.
> Fires burn faster, the winds fly drier, a people's anger spirals
> swifter in the dust of those miniature devil-winds building up
> into the cyclone that must sweep off their oppressors.[11]

The younger ideologues...those hankering after the Marxist-socialist utopia of a class-less society--ally with the masses and like Soyinka, urge a revolution that would cleanse society of its present ills and usher all into nirvana. These ideologues see literature as an instrument of liberation from the oppressors who invariably belong to the ruling class, urging the masses to rise up and overthrow the oppressive system. In Iyayi's *Heroes,* the protagonist urges a third army to rise up and liberate the cheated and betrayed masses, while Osofisan in *Once Upon Four Robbers* creates hoodlums who are bent, Robinhood-style, on forcible redistribution of the nation's wealth, by robbing the rich and sharing the loot among themselves who represent the

---

[11] Wole Soyinka, *Season of Anomy.* London: Thomas Nelson and Sons, (1980), pp.92, 111

masses.

But with the antennae of current works by Iyayi, Odia Ofeimun, Sowande, Osofisan, and Omotoso pointing toward revolutionary trends, Achebe's mature vision in *The Anthills of the Savannah* urges reform rather than revolution, the consequences of which might be cataclysmic. We might need to heed this voice of the elder:

> Experience and intelligence warn us that man's progress in freedom will be piecemeal, slow and undramatic. Revolution may be necessary for taking a society out of an intractable stretch of quagmire, but it does not confer freedom, and may indeed hinder it ...reform may be a dirty word then but it begins to look more and more like the most promising route to success in the world.[12]

II

So, as we turn our attention briefly from the writers to their products, we may ask: what has literature done for Nigeria, for instance? Why does it deserve a place in the scheme of things in our educational system? Well, we may ask: has it ever occurred to any one of us that while technology could be "transferred", literature and the arts belong uniquely to a people. Literature, like tradition and culture is autochthonous; and if we allow literature and the arts to die through neglect, our very humanity, our identity as a people will not only be under threat but it will disappear and our very identity in world culture will face complete effacement. Nigeria, of course, need no longer entertain any such fears. We are not only the pathfinders in African literature; we are the undisputed leaders in that field. Our literatures have

---

[12] Chinua Achebe. *Anthills of the Savannah.* Ibadan: Heinemann, (1999), p.99.

indeed fostered national consciousness, patriotism and nationalism. Every Nigerian holds his head high anywhere in the world because Achebe, Okara, Soyinka, Ola Rotimi, Niyi Osundare, Festus Iyayi, Ken Saro-Wiwa and Ben Okri are indigenes of this great country of literary giants. Nigeria's most valued export commodity is not petroleum products but her literatures which have won every imaginable international prize including the Nobel Prize. Achebe's works alone, by the latest count, have been translated into fifty different languages outside Africa. Through her literatures as mentioned above, Nigeria exports her culture and traditions to other parts of the world and, through these literary works, exposes to the world the very foundations of her national consciousness.

At the level of society, the aesthetic experience fosters mutual sympathy and understanding which will normally help on a larger scale to draw men together, to draw our country together, since all shared experience helps to bring people together in friendship and mutual respect, for any group of people who share the same aesthetic experience have a bond between them and feel united under a common identity. So, Nigerian literatures unite Nigerians more than politics or science or religion. This is true of any nation. Nigeria today stands tall before the international community because of the collective endeavours of her writers. While our politics and the shenanigans of our business deals most often sell Nigeria's private shames in the international scandal market, it is through the collective endeavours of Nigerian writers that Nigeria stands redeemed and enhanced in the eyes of the world, since the onus of moral regeneration in our society has always lain with our writers, as if in response to Nietzsche's call that "society needs an elite that will set a pattern and curb the thoughtlessness of the masses."

Nigerian writers have accomplished this by establishing what I refer to as the Nigerian tradition in literature--a tradition that has set a pattern for the entire continent. It is that tradition which makes use of and expresses allegiance to our folk culture by creatively making use of our proverbs, local myths, folk tales, *et cetera,* in giving expression to our national culture by stridently stressing what is indigenous to Nigeria. Tutuola, Achebe, Soyinka, Elechi Amadi, Okigbo, Ola Rotimi, and many others were all concerned with cultural assertion and were pioneers in what we have come to regard as cultural nationalism in Nigerian literature: in their stressing the innate dignity of the Nigerian, in their concern with the rehabilitation of the image of the black man in general, and the Nigerian man and woman in particular--that image damaged and distorted by white writers. They have all established this tradition mainly through myth--making, through the mythopoeia of group identity and group experience, thereby transmitting culture, pursuing an ideology of cultural renaissance, emphasizing our communal and collective philosophy, stressing the success stories or failures of communities rather than the fortunes or misfortunes of the individual, calling attention to a rural rather than an industrial or technological way of life that has led to a fulfilled way of existence. They have done this by bending, twisting and proverbializing the English language or revealing the innate wealth of our vernacular languages.

The Negritude movement as I had said elsewhere, had a catalytic effect on African literature. It was the centre piece of Africa's literary nationalism in the wake of political independence for all black peoples. To regain cultural initiative, to imbue political independence with national and cultural pride, to embark on the path of psychic reconstruction, were what energized the literary movement known as Negritude. Negritude, what Jean Paul Sartre calls "an antiracist racism" was embarked upon by writers of African descent as a form of literary therapy for the common welfare of all peoples of African descent to recover their essential selfhood bashed and mutilated by white arrogance through the colonial intrusion."

We have dwelt on Achebe and the Negritude movement to point to the function of literature, as a branch of the arts, in the cultural development of our people. We have also touched on history as an aid in this journey to heal our wounded psyche, in restoring a sense of dignity and pride to a people denigrated as irrelevant in the march of civilization. Here also, we recall our dramatists - Rotimi, in *Kurunmi* and *Ovanranwen Nogbaisi,* Soyinka in *Death and the King's Horseman,* Osofisan in *Morountodun* all have reflected our past through projection and criticism of our national heroes by highlighting the strengths and weaknesses in the characters of our past from whom we learn the appropriate lesson in order to steer our ship of state to a better course. And through translations into various European and Asian languages, our literatures have gone international and have helped us carve out a definite niche in world culture. Our folklore, our manner of dress, our customs--all have permeated world culture through the collective endeavours of our writers.

In the light of the above, it becomes clear that Nigeria has definitely benefited, has definitely developed, has definitely become a more modern, a more stable society through the collective endeavours of our artists, through the collective contributions made in the realm of the arts. We cannot say this about our endeavours in the realm of science and technology on which the Federal Government has pitched her tent, if we just cast a glance in the region of her lopsided J.A.M.B admission policy in favour of science and technology. Need we then be reminded that the arts make for order, for discipline, for refinement, for unity?

If, as we all agree, language is the bedrock of civilization and culture and is fundamental to the existence of human societies, we would appreciate the more its importance in Nigeria, which is a country still striving after legitimacy as a nation. By an accident of history, English men and the English language may have made the existence of Nigeria as a geographical entity possible, English may be the official language of Nigeria and most of our internationally recognized writers write in English. But for our own cultural and national development, must we remain condemned in the use of that language which reminds us of our bondage to the imperial legacy of colonialism? To assume a language, it is agreed, is to assume a world view, to assume the cultural view of the owners of that language.

In our literature written in English, we recognize the gymnastic volleyball our writers have played with that language. According to Achebe, English in the hands of our writers has surrendered itself to all kinds of use; it has been bent, proverbialized, pidginized, domesticated, even vernacularised. But it is still the English language. If we can communicate easily in it with Ghanaians and Camerounians, where then does it acquire this divine afflatus to weld us together as a nation, as different from a mere geographical entity? Granted, we can do little to dismiss the use of the English language in the immediate future, but knowing the importance of language in nation-building, must the Nigerian nation surrender itself to an eternal bondage to the English language? We cannot continue to discuss literature without discussing issues of its language. These issues are necessary in the light of the Nigerian Government's language policy. True, use of the mother-tongue is encouraged in the early years of primary school, but this piece-meal approach to the language question will never build a strong, virile, patriotic, united Nigerian citizenry. Nigeria should make it compulsory for every Nigerian child to pass at the school certificate level, his mother-tongue and at least one other major language in Nigeria, and this would influence posting during the Youth Corps to consolidate the language learned in school, in the manner in which students of foreign languages spend a year abroad to consolidate knowledge of the language learnt by rote in school.

In effect, a young Nigerian, if this suggestion is adopted, can influence his posting during his service year by the language he studied in school. An Ijaw should study either Hausa or Yoruba; a Hausa, either Igbo or Yoruba, *et cetera*. The present haphazard language policy does not have the building of one nation in mind.

And if we have not given up the idea of developing an indigenous technology (not a transferred one), we should pay urgent and insistent attention to the development of indigenous languages. A young Japanese student revealed recently that in looking over undergraduate notes taken by his ancestors in Japanese universities since the 1850s, he noted that his grandfather took all his notes in English, his father half in English and half in Japanese, and his own notes are completely in Japanese. And Japan, today, has a very strong indigenous technology--a technological base that is now the envy of Europe and America.

How does this affect us in Nigeria? Well, Nigeria wants a "transfer" rather than a development of indigenous technology by re-enforcing rather than discouraging the study of English at every stage of a youth's development. Secondly, the study of our indigenous language has suffered benign neglect through inadequate funding, lack of sponsorship of indigenous language newspapers and publications of books in the vernacular. One has no choice but urge urgent government attention to the development of languages and literatures in the mother-tongue and making compulsory, the study and passing of a major second Nigerian language by all Nigerian Youths at the School Certificate level, because knowledge and development of the mother-tongue is a major vehicle of acculturation and will help advance the cause of national unity and cultural identity. Furthermore, as Nnabuenyi Ugonna urges:

> Our technological revolution will continue to elude us so long as we fail to indigenise our technological language,

Because

> It is needful to stress here that in the African context, to make the scientific process fully understandable entails the imparting of science literacy in the indigenous language understood by the vast majority of people. Foreign technological language is so esoteric to a vast majority of the people that the hope of achieving an appreciable level of scientific literacy in it, is merely day-dreaming.[13]

This paper has argued that Nigeria's literatures have contributed immensely to her cultural and national development. Nigerian writers have won her international fame and have placed Nigeria firmly on the literary map of the world. Her dramatists have helped to re-establish the African personality through cultural reaffirmation. Her historians have corrected the distortions about Africa's place in world history denied us by Europeans, and, as we have just stated above, we only now need a clear language policy in our educational endeavours to weld this country together

---

[13] Nnabuenyi Ugonna, "Language and African Technological Development," in The Humanities and National Development in Nigeria ed. A.E. Erevbetine and Nina Mba (Lagos: Nelson publisher), pp. 167, 179.

into a nation that is more united and more unified.

And one should not leave the Nigerian female writer out of this discourse. Again it is the Nigerian female writer, Flora Nwapa, who set the pace both for Nigeria and the entire continent as the trailblazer in modern African female fiction writing, and is therefore historically important. She saw it as her duty to redeem and correct the disparaged and debased image of the Nigerian woman as the women saw it depicted by male writers like Achebe and Cyprian Ekwensi--women destined in the words of Chikwenye Ogunyemi "to carry *foofoo* and soup to men discussing 'important matters.'"14 Nwapa set the pace for the feminist trend in Nigerian literature, quickly joined by Buchi Emecheta, Zulu Sofola, Zaynab Alkali, Ifeoma Okoye, and a host of others, by preaching the dignity and economic independence of the Nigerian woman in captivating titles like *Women Are Different* (Nwapa) and *Double Yoke* (Emecheta). Far from being parasites, far from being dependent on their men, the feminist Nigerian woman is highlighted as dignified in comportment, economically independent, highly industrious and possessing superior and higher moral values than her male counterparts. Through their writings, the image of the Nigerian woman as equal in all respects with her male counterparts, is now firmly established.

In sum, the writer is a patriot who, for love of his country has taken great risks to ensure that we live in a free and democratic society where no one is oppressed. The ultimate end toward which the writer tends is utopia, for whether the writer is revolutionary or reformist in orientation, every writer is essentially a dreamer envisaging a heaven on earth, freedom from racial, colonial and neo-colonial abuse, in

---

14 Chikwenye Ogunyemi, "Women and Nigerian Literature", in Perspectives on Nigerian Literature, Vol. I, Lagos: Guardian Books (Nigeria) Ltd.,(1988), p. 6

short, a golden era of opportunities. Writers are finally the interpreters of our culture, the enemy of sinister forces in society, the conserver of our values, the terror of bad governments. "Force and right are the governors of this world; force, till right is ready", says Jourbert. And force is the terror of all writers. That is why writing may be a hazardous profession and one could die in the cause of that calling.

In the light of the foregoing, Nigeria should realize that it is not through science, technology, and politics but through our literatures that she gained international attention, fame, and respect. We, therefore, urge the federal government of Nigeria to:

1. Name streets, public squares, and airports after Nigeria's great writers, not just after politicians, and the military elite as has hitherto been the practice;

2. Fund the publications of the Nigerian Academy of Letters;

3. Establish and fund the post of writer-in-residence or artist-in-residence for our most eminent writers and artists in designated universities to demonstrate to our young men and women that there are other avenues to fame than just the area of politics;

4. To build for the Nigerian Academy of Letters a permanent secretariat along with a well-funded, well-maintained writers and artists village attached to it, where symposia, workshops, and seminars are held. That should be part of Nigeria's national monuments and legacies; and

5. To establish and fund, as in England, the post of poet-laureate to one eminent writer for a life time to encourage our young writers to aspire to that position of eminence.

Achebe in his Nigerian National Order of Merit Lecture captioned "What Has Literature Got to Do with it?" tells us that a nation becomes what it honours and how it does it is a paradigm of its national style. Nigeria does not even pretend to honour knowledge in the same way it regularly honours its politicians through public monuments. In the light of this, the federal government is urged to do the above as a token of her recognition of the importance of literature in national development. Nigeria, which has never batted an eyelid in building houses and naming streets after mere teenage footballers, has never seen it fit to extend that sort of courtesy to our eminent writers and world-class intellectuals. You are now quite familiar with public squares, streets, and barracks named after the military elite and politicians. But have you ever heard of even a side-street at Abuja named after Kenneth Dike, Biobaku, Achebe, Soyinka, Gabriel Okara, Elechi Amadi or any other intellectual? Even at state or local government levels, writers and intellectuals are thoroughly ignored. This is not the practice in the civilized world. Does it imply that Nigeria refuses to give that nod which we all give to knowledge? Does it further mean that Nigeria has refused to join the habits and practices of civilized communities?

Achebe is dead right: A nation becomes what it honours. And how she does it becomes a paradigm of her national style. Nigeria needs to demonstrate to the world that it values knowledge by also honouring her eminent writers and intellectuals.

4

Morning Yet On Criticism Day: the criticism of African literature in the twentieth century*

Ex *Africa Semper Aliquid Novi* (Cicero)[1]
Criticism like manure smells bad, but it helps writers to grow.[2]

Africa's contact with Europe has not always *been* an unhappy one. How did the continent of African get its name? After the third Punic War (between Rome and Carthage), Scipio Africanus, a Roman General was mandated to police the South Mediterranean Sea, especially the present North West Africa (Libya, Tunisia, Algeria,) and anyone venturing into those sea coasts was said to be going to Africanus land. In time, "Africanus land" applied to the whole continent and to Cicero, the great Roman orator, Africa was a constant source of wonder and mystery, hence, his quip which acts as a superscript for this study.

Africa's second contact with Europe in the nineteenth century (the Berlin Conference 1884-1885) which gave European powers "areas of influence" brought Nigeria under the British imperial hegemony. This was a mixed blessing:

* Nigerian National Merit Award, Award Winner's Lecture, Abuja, December 2009.
[1] Quoted by Taban Lo Liyong, "Dark Areas in African Studies: Inaugural Lecture, University of Venda, South Africa (May 22, 1996), 1, 24.
[2] Charles E. Nnolim in *Sunday Vanguard* (September 7, 1997) p. 25.

Nigeria became a subject people under colonial rule but she gained a world language that gave us a shared heritage with Europe and the rest of the world. With the English language came its literature and with its literature we gained access to world civilization. And with access to English and European literatures came knowledge of their critical skills and methodology.

What is literature?

Those of us addicted to, or specialized in the humane letters regard literature mainly as imaginative writing...that writing which is more emotionally moving than intellectually instructive; that writing which primarily deals with a make believe world; that writing whose language is highly connotative rather than denotative, symbolic rather than literal, figurative rather than plain; that writing we regard as "verbal works of art", that writing that is remarked by its fictionality and imaginative import; that writing in which ideas are wrapped up in symbols, images, concepts; that writing which normally catapults us into another world of appearance and reality through the powers of the imagination. I also define as literature writing in which the aesthetic function dominates; writing in which the ultimate aim of the author is to produce an object of art.

To enter this world and enjoy it, we must come with what Coleridge calls "that willing suspension of disbelief which constitutes poetic faith" for we must be prepared to believe that in this world, flowers "smile" in the sunshine, and animals talk like men. When we enter this other world, we must relax, for we are prepared to be entertained, for we read literature primarily for its entertainment value.

Part of the entertainment afforded by literature is embedded in its use of very refined language, what is referred to as "the right words in the right order", or, as

Alexander Pope puts it:

> What oft was thought
> But ne'er so well expressed

Literature exists, in the main, to entertain us, and by entertaining us it enriches our leisure hours and offers us pleasure.

Literature, we all can now appreciate is a humanistic discipline, for its province is the improvement of man's lot on earth. Do you remember Alexander Pope's advice:

> Know thyself, presume not God to scan
>
> The proper study of mankind is man.

Literature as art deploys language embellished with pleasurable accessories, to paraphrase Aristotle... and it is around the embellished use of language that the creative energy of the story deploys itself. And to invest the story with meaning, there must be some truth about life, something to chew over, some theme, some moral, some philosophy of life, and some metaphor of life that tugs at the edges of a symbol. As in all art, literature is useful, for as art, it is not a waste of time. Horace tells us that literature exists to delight and to teach *(dulce et utile)*.

Criticism and the critic

Art unaccompanied by criticism is dead art. Critics keep asking questions about the arts: What is art? What is its use? Why is art created? Why is it studied? Is it good or bad art? And what is the influence of art (or literature for that matter) on humanity? Furthermore, how art influences us has always engaged the efforts of critics, preachers, teachers, governments, moralists, and parents. The study of how literature and the arts influence mankind, belongs to the affective theory of art: how art moves us, convinces us, causes riots, makes us angry or makes us laugh or weep, leads to immorality or even makes governments imprison artists or seize artefacts. These reveal to us the power of art. And this is where criticism and the critic come in.

The function of the critic is both judicial and social. It is also interventionist. His function is to estimate and pass judgment on the value and quality of the work of art before him, he is a mediator between the specialist and the layman, between the work of art and its readership or the audience. The critic's social function is, therefore, to be of some use to the reader in helping the reader understand the work in question. It is the duty of the critic also to arouse enthusiasm for the work by getting the reader buy and read the work. A sound critic must, above all, be objective and detached.

Critics are defenders of poets, and the commentators on their works; to illustrate obscure beauties; to place some passages in a better light; to redeem writers from malicious interpretations, to help out an author's modesty who is not ostentatious of his wit; in short to shield him from the ill nature of those fellows who take upon themselves the venerable name of censors.

The word "criticism" comes from the Greek word "Krinein" to judge, to discern. Criticism can also be defined as the art of judging or evaluating the beauties and the faults in a work of art objectively, without partiality, without the intrusion of our personal feelings, personal liking or disliking of either the work or its author. As just mentioned, criticism sets out to find out: what is art, what is its use; why is it studied; why is art created; is it good or bad art. In other words, criticism exists:

To defend literature and justify its existence. Sir Philip Sidney wrote *An Apology for Poetry* in 1595 in reply to Stephen Gosson who in 1585 published the *School of Abuse* in which he asserted that drama encouraged prostitution, pick-pocketing, gambling and other tavern sins. In 1607, Samuel Daniel wrote *Defence of Rhyme* in answer to Thomas Watson who regarded poetry as a barbaric invention of the middle ages. In 1821, Shelley wrote his famous *A Defence of Poetry* in answer to Thomas Love Peacock who published *The Four Ages of Poetry,* which predicted the decline of poetry with the advancement of science and technology.

Criticism legislates taste and sets the standard. This is its prescriptive function. Horace (65 B.C) in *The Art of Poetry* discussed the unities in drama and decorum in the action of characters. A giant, he said, should not speak like a dwarf nor should a servant behave or speak like a king.

Criticism acts as a guide to writers and exists to aid, guide, advise an author where he is going wrong. Criticism further exists to interpret, explain, explicate, analyse a work of art, to mediate between the specialist and the amateur, between the work and its audience. It is also another function of criticism to protect the reader from poor or bad works and to promote and recommend good ones; and also propagate, according to Arnold the best that is known and thought in existing works of art. Other subtle functions of criticism must be mentioned:

- To demonstrate the application (in practice) of the principles of good writing and to expound the theories guiding literature in order to show the reader the processes by which literature is created, also to show the processes by which literature affects the mind, and demonstrate the principles that guide creative writing.
- To serve the major function of appreciation through judicial criticism, it is the duty of criticism to address itself to such questions of value as:

a.   Is the work good i.e. is it ethical, honourable, excellent, fine, beneficial and does it have worth and quality:

b.   Is it true or is it a true representation of what it sets out to recreate, i.e. does it have verisimilitude, authenticity, accuracy, validity. Can it stand any appropriate test?

c.   Is it beautiful, i.e. does it have charm, grace, artistry, symmetry, proportion, polish, and refinement? The above is what art aspires to: the good, the true, and the beautiful. These are the absolute values.

When Chinua Achebe, the renowned writer and novelist won the Nigerian National Order of Merit Award, he delivered a lecture captioned "What Has Literature Got to Do with it." As a critic, my question is "what has criticism got to do with it"? The "it" I suppose, refers to works of art in general and to literature in particular. By getting the reader buy and read the work. A sound critic must, above all, be objective and detached.

A critic actually is like a plumber in the area of literary creativity. And plumbing is considered a lowly occupation. It was Disraeli who quipped: you know what the critics are: the men who have failed in literature and art.[3] Henry Wotton tells us: critics are brushers of noble men's clothers.[4] He is further supported by Coleridge who refers to critics as:

> People who would have been poets, historians, biographers...
> if they could. They have tried their talents at one or the other,
> and have failed; therefore they turn to criticism.[5]

I must humbly submit that I am a failed artist. In all

[3] For Notes 3, 4, 5, in this study, see James Reeves, The critical Sense. London (1985), 7-9.

[4] Quoted by S. T. Coleridge in T. S. Dorsey (ed), On the Art of Classical Literary Criticism. London, Penguin (1965) 87 -- 88.

[5] Quoted by S. T. Coleridge in T. S. Dorsey (ed), On the Art of Classical Literary Criticism. London, Penguin (1965) 87 -- 88

these thirty odd years of teaching literature at the University level, I have written only two published short stories and couple of poems. If I have not learnt by now that I am no Achebe or Osundare or Ngugi wa Thiong'o, then I must be the greatest fool alive.

But deep in my heart, I know, that the critic does not occupy a position so lowly as great writers make his functions seem. Horace comes to my aid here:

> So, I will play the part of the whetstone, which can put on a blade, though it is not itself capable of cutting. Even if I write nothing myself, I will teach the poet his duties and obligations. I will tell him where to find his resources, what will nourish his poetic art, what he may or may not do with propriety, where the right cause will take him and where the wrong.[6]

It is unarguable that criticism has given direction and purpose to African literature in the twentieth century following the emergence of gifted and serious writers led by Achebe, Ngugi wa Thiong'o and many others. Critics like Emmanuel Obiechina drew attention to the idea of cultural nationalism in African literature culminating in the part the negritude movement played in the rehabilitation of the African personality.

Towards the Decolonization of African Literature (1980)[7] by Chinweizu, Jemie and Madubuike alerted African readers and critics to the fact that African critics tended to ape colonialist writers in thinking that African literature is a mere extension of European literature and urged them to change direction by insisting on the autochthony of African literature. Critics like Emenyonu frontally attacked expatriate critics like Lindfors and Gerald Moore who kept

---

[6] Quoted by S. T. Coleridge in T. S. Dorsey (ed), On the Art of Classical Literary Criticism. London, Penguin (1965) 87 -- 88

[7] Chinweizu, *et al.* Toward the Decolonization of African Literature, Enugu, Fourth Dimension (1980).

insisting that writers like Achebe, Ekwensi, and Tutuola always drew their inspiration from European writers and even copied these European writers.

It was literary criticism by African scholars that eventually shaped the nature of African literature as we have it today. It was criticism by African critics that began the debate on the African aesthetic in literature... its oral base, its use of African mythology as quarry; its folk tradition, its literature of colonial experience; its literature of apartheid; the problem of language-use in African literature; its generic uniqueness. In my own modest contribution, I have drawn attention to the unhappy nature of African literature in the last century and the narrowness of its canvas. It was a weeping literature, a literature of lamentation over the wounds inflicted on all Africans through slavery and colonialism. We now owe it to criticism to pose challenges for our writers in the future.

II

We now turn serious attention to the main concern of this lecture, the criticism of African literature in the twentieth century. In the twentieth century, African literature was at the gate of a new dawn. And writing on new literatures required special insights and sound training. The pioneers of the criticism of African literature in the twentieth century faced daunting tasks since a new literature demands new critical approaches. The critical problems faced by indigenous African critics in the twentieth century were, among others:

a. Its definition, especially the adventitious nature of African literature.
b. its newness
c. its oral base

d. what critical standards to adopt — Western, Universal or indigenous?
e. Its uniqueness
f. The problem of its appropriate language
g. Its proper aesthetics\
h. Who is the appropriate audience of African literature
i. What appropriate ideology
j. Who should be its accredited critic
k. The problem of source and influence
l. The problem of lack of distance between the work and its critics; between the writer and his critic.
m. The future of African literature.

The above is already a mouthful, but we start with the oral base. Since Pio Zirimu coined the word orature to encompass much of African's oral-based literature, African experts of oral literature helped to recognize its study under schematized headings:

i. Spoken: proverbs, riddles, myths, legends, incantations, etc.
ii. Sung: work songs, dirges, elegies, war songs, lampoons, birth songs, hunting songs, lullabies.
iii. Acted: rituals, festivals initiations, observances, dances, masquerades

Indigenous African critics established that the uniqueness of African literature takes its shape from its orature, its oral-based origins, its orality; its myth-making. Tutuola's works come to mind. And Soyinka had engaged this aspect of African literature in *Myth and Culture in African literature*.

It came as a complete surprise to the Western critic that when the African critic woke up to take control of the criticism of his own literatures, he started angrily by attacking expatriate critics whom, he believed, brought their supercilious and arrogant attitudes to bear on all things African, including African literatures. In *African Literature Today*, No. 5. 1971, with the spirited lead article by Ernest Emenyonu captioned "African Literature: What Does it Take to be Its Critic?[8] the author's righteous indignation and the debate surrounding it may have finally silenced expatriate critics such as Judith Gleason and Margaret Laurence, but if failed to daunt the main object of its attack Bernth Lindfors, who came up with a taunting response in *African Literature Today*, No. 7, 1975.[9] In "the Blind Men and the Elephant," Lindfors warned xenophobic champions of criticism of African literature that "common sense just does not allow a single tribe of critics to claim a monopoly on clear vision" and that "indeed, if all interpretation were left to native critics, truth might be sought principally on a local level, its universal dimensions all but forgotten" (54).

The issue which Emenyonu's article spearheaded was the question of identity for Africans and the authenticity of their literatures. Emenyonu's open resentment was against "colonialist critics" whose hobbyhorse was finding "masters" for African writers, attempting in the process to overturn the "depreciation of the African image" by expatriate critics. He went for Lindfors jugular, Lindfors, who asserted that Cyprian Ekwensi obtained his stimulation from third-rate American movies and fourth-rate British and American paperback novels," preferring that no "literary godfathers" outside Africa be found for African writers." Ayi Kwei Armah attacked Charles Larson *(The Emergence of African Fiction),* accusing him of "Larsony" or the use of fiction in the criticism of fiction", while others descended on Gerald

---

[8] Ernest Emenyonu, "African Literature: What Does it take to be its Critic?" ALT, 5 (1971).

[9] Bernth Lindfors, "The Blind Men and the Elephant" ALT, 7 (1975).

Moore *(Seven African Writers)* for tracing Tutuola's masters to Dante, Bunyan, and Blake; Achebe's to Joseph Conrad, and Soyinka's, Clark's and Okara's (poets all) to Hopkins, Eliot, Yeats, Dylan Thomas, and others. And the gentle Achebe had grumbled about "getting a little weary of all the special kinds of criticism which have been designed for us by people whose knowledge of us is very limited."[10]

But the finishing blow which ended the attacks on colonialist criticism and the expatriates came from the most influential book on the criticism of African literature of the period: Toward the *Decolonization of African Literature* (Enugu: Fourth Dimension Publishers, 1980) by the maverick critics Chinweizu, Jemie, and Madubuike. In language as crude and vulgar as their adopted "Bolekaja" stance, they asserted that the cultural task in hand is to end all foreign domination of African culture" and to probe "the ways and means whereby western imperialism has maintained its hegemony over African literature" (i, xiii). They went further, insisting that African literature is not and should never be made to be an extension of European literature, either in form or content; that foreign forms and metaphors should be expunged from the corpus of African Literature; and that those who interpret African literature as an extension of European literature are traitors chasing after foreign literary gods.

The major achievement of Toward the *Decolonization of African Literature,* what was new, what made it such an influential book — was the attention they turned to African writers and critics who mimicked and copied European literary modes and writers. Not satisfied with attacking colonialist and expatriate critics (who were already receiving

---

[10] "Where Angels Fear to Tread", Morning Yet on Creation Day. London; Heinemann, (1975), 46.

hammer blows from Emenyonu *et al.*), Chinweizu and company went for the throats of fellow African writers and critics in an effort to complete the task of fully decolonizing African literature. They asserted that the literature written by African writers was "the literature of imitation and adaptation, not a literature of imagination and invention."

In what was clearly a case of overkill, the authors drew our awareness to how deeply and pervasively most indigenous African writers and critics were tied to the European literary apron strings, how they were never weaned away from the European literary breast. This is where *Toward the Decolonization of African Literature* carved its niche in the annals of criticism of African literature in their efforts to finally cure African literature and its indigenous writers and critics of their colonial hangover. After the troika, the debate over the influence of expatriate criticism of African literature died completely. And the time had arrived which justified Joseph Okpaku's insistence that the primary criticism of African art must come from Africans using African standards.

Prominent among the journals which debated critical issues that shaped African literature in the twentieth century were *African literature Today, Research in African Literatures, Black Orpheus, Transition, Matatu, Okike, Kunapipi*, and a host of in-house journals emanating from various English and literature departments of African universities.

But all the debates in these various journals never resolved the burning question of what constitutes the African aesthetic in literature, what makes African literature so unique that one could easily distinguish it from other world literatures. The various debates, on-going and unabating, seem to have gravitated around certain key ideas that remind us of various exclamations of the blind men and the elephant. Critics argue vigorously about the accuracy of their perspicacious insights, but the issue of an African aesthetic in literature remains largely unresolved. And the issue may remain unresolved in spite of the amount of ink spilt on what constitutes African literature and its definition, on the "newness" of African literature on the world scene; on the problem of the appropriate language suitable for its propagation (European or indigenous); on who constitutes the audience of that literature, on its oral base or orature; on the critical standards by which it should be judged; on who should be its accredited critics (indigenous critics or European); on its ideological orientation; on what constitutes its appropriate theory; and on the function of African literature (utilitarian or aesthetic); on its Negritude aesthetic. These unresolved issues were the main critical preoccupations of the 1980s.[11]

Toward the Decolonization of African Literature, as I mentioned earlier, addressed the issue of the African aesthetic in literature by drawing our attention to how deeply Eurocentric rather than Afrocentric our African critics and writers were. The major flaw in their thesis was the myopic view that their work was done once African literature and criticism were decolonized. Their avowed irreverence and quarrelsome stance failed to address where we went from there once we ceased to be Eurocentric, or in what new directions in the theory of African literature we

---

[11] For the various Studies reflecting the African Aesthetics in Literature, see
1. Joseph Okpaku: "Tradition, Culture, and Criticism" Presence Africaine, No 70 (1969).
2. Obi Wali, "The Dead End of African Literature"Transition, No. 10 (1963)
3. Stanley Macebuh, "African Aesthetics in Traditional African Art" Okike, No. 5 (1975).
4. Dan Lzevbaye, "The State of Criticism in African Literature" ALT, No. 7 (1975).
5. Isidore Okpewho. "The Aesthetics of Old African Art". Okike, No. 8 (1975).
6. Charles E. Nnolim, "An African Literary Aesthetic: A Prolegomenon "Ba Shiru, vol. 7, No. 2 (1976).

should turn. A few other attempts, most of them unsuccessful, were made in the late 1970s and the early 1980s to address the question of the African-aesthetic in literature. The most uncoordinated of these efforts was a medley of unrelated and misaddressed essays edited by Lemuel Johnson *et al.* entitled *Toward Defining the African Aesthetic* (1982). Most others took the traditional view summarizable in the words of Kwasi Wiredu:

> African nationalists in search of an African identity, Afro-Americans in search of their African roots, and foreigners in search of exotic diversion... all demand an African Philosophy fundamentally different from Western Philosophy, even if it means the familiar witches' brew. *(Philosophy and African Culture.* Cambridge, Cambridge University Press, 1980, p. 30).

In the above is the circumambient presence of the Negritude aesthetic, a movement that is now behind us but which constituted a vital road through which all people of African descent had to pass in their collective search for authenticity and the restoration of the innate dignity of the African personality. But since the informing spirit of the Negritude aesthetic in African literature is Africa's continuing search for identity, that movement may be behind us but not quite forgotten in our many-sided approach to autochthony. Respect for our identity was uppermost in Emenyonu's mind when he asked Lindfors to cease searching for literary godfathers for our writers. It was uppermost in the troika's minds when they roundly condemned Adrian Roscoe and others as expatriate critics who are denigrating the genuine Africanness of our literatures while they turned around to condemn fellow African writers who were Eurocentric in their output.

The Negritude aesthetic still hovers around our

continuing debate about language-use in our literatures. It seems now axiomatic that so long as we don't forget our colonial past, so long shall the African personality hang on to the Negritude aesthetic as a reassuring counterweight.

As debate around the Negritude aesthetic waned what may mildly be termed "oppositional criticism" arose. A group of ideologues, critics brandishing the sociological-cum-Marxist wand announced their presence. They arrived with enough revolutionary fervour to make the masses aware of their downtrodden status and the inequalities in their society to, if possible, effect a social revolution. These radical voices, engaged in discursive relations between classes in their theoretical constructs, politicized the cultural basis on which the criticism of African criticism was hitherto based. One has in mind the rise of a group of younger writers-cum-critics who initially came together as the "Komfess Artistes" comprising Femi Osofisan, Kole Omotoso, Bode Sowande and Biodun Jeyifo. Their critical journal was *Positive Review* and their rambunctious student, Chidi Amuta, published *The Theory of African Literature* which brilliantly encapsulated the major Marxist theories on which their sociological approach to interpreting African literature was hinged. The proletarian propensities of these critics including G. G. Darah, Yemi Ogunbiyi and Eddie Madunagu found their critical quarry in the works of their fellow radical writers: Festus Iyayi (Violence), Femi Osofisan (Kolera Kolej) and outside Nigeria, Ousmane Sembene's *God's Bits of Wood* and Ngugi wa Thiong'o's works, especially *Petals of Blood* and *Devil on the Cross*. Although radical writers and critics brought new tools for interpreting the Marxist-socialist approaches to literature, the Marxist-Socialist approach hardly led to any new revolutionary rationalities among the African proletariat, judging from the viewpoint that the ultimate aim of the

Marxist-Socialist ideologue was utopian: to reorder society so that the dictatorship of the proletariat would take root on the African soil. The idea of criticism as class-warfare did not quite succeed.

Feminist criticism of African literature made its own impact. It was an ideology, of a different hue imported from Europe. In simple terms, feminism urges recognition of the claims by women for equal rights with men: legal, political, economic, social, and marital. Chikwenye Ogunyemi, Rose Acholonu, Chioma Opara... all were young critics who, taking her their cue from female writers led by Flora Nwapa, Mariama Ba and others like Ama Ata Aidoo and Zaynab Alkali undertook to redeem and correct through criticism, the image of women as depicted by male writers like Chinua Achebe and Cyprian Ekwensi. As these female critics saw it, male writers see and depict women as dependent, helpless, good time girls, or mere prostitutes and concubines or "kept women" destined in the words of Ogunyemi "to carry *foofoo* and soup to men discussing important matters."[12]

The female critics ably demonstrated -that far from being parasites, far from being dependent or subservient to men, the African, nay Nigerian woman has dignity, is economically independent and industrious and possesses higher moral authority than their male counterparts. In the end, the female critics succeeded, by the end of the twentieth century, in establishing that the image of the Nigerian woman was equal in all respects to their male counterparts.

The twentieth century saw the beginnings of written literature and its attendant criticism in Africa. Both writers and critics were on a pioneering mission. It is impossible for the critics to make predictions of what trends criticism will

---

[12] Chikwenye Ogunyemi, "Women and Nigerian Literature," Perspectives on Nigerian Literature: Lagos, Guardian Books (1988), 66.

take ahead of the creative writers. The wind follows the sun, we learn in geography lessons just as 'trends in criticism inevitably follow trends in creative writing. It can never be vice-versa.

As for written African literature in the twentieth century this critic made certain observations:

> That African literature in the 20ᵗʰ century was not a happy one: it was lachrymal; it was a literature of lamentation, a weeping literature following Africa's unhappy experience with slavery and colonialism.[13]

Having lost her pride through slavery and colonialism, modern African literature arose from the ashes of her past experiences. It became a literature with a strong sense of loss; loss of our dignity; loss of our culture and tradition; loss of our religion, loss of our land; loss of our very humanity. Any wonder that the titles of our most celebrated literary works highlighted these losses. Have we forgotten Achebe's *Things Fall Apart;* Ngugi wa Thiongo's *Weep Not Child;* Alan Paton's *Cry the Beloved Country?* And protest literature over Apartheid further irrigated Africa's tears because of man's inhumanity to man, to a people dubbed the wretched of the earth. It is hard to forget these words from Alan Paton:

> Sadness falls upon them all. Sadness and fear and hate, how they well up in the heart and mind, whenever one opens the pages of these messengers of doom. Cry, the beloved country, these things are not yet an end; the sun pours down on the earth; on the lovely land that man cannot enjoy. He only knows the fear of his heart.[14]

---

[13] Charles E. Nnolim. "The Nigerian Tradition in the Novel." Commonwealth Novel in English, vol. 11, No. 2 (July 1983), 22-40.

[14] Alan Paton, *Cry The Beloved Country*. New York, Scribner's (1948), 73-74.

This critic had observed that African writers in the twentieth century were not imaginatively daring and this resulted in the narrowness of their canvas. The major reason was the defensive nature of our written literature much of which was the pre-occupation of our literature with re-establishing the "African personality" and restoring the dignity of the African man bruised and damaged by slavery and colonialism. It was observed that the European writer belonged to a minority race with a superiority complex and was more imaginatively daring and expansive than this African counterpart who seemed to display a defensive and inferiority complex by confining his creative literary output to the African soil.[15]

Let me explain. The European writer of the nineteenth and twentieth centuries set his sights beyond Europe. Rider Haggard's *King Solomon's Mines,* Orwell's *Burmese Days,* E. M. Forster's *A Passage to India.* Conrad's *Heart of Darkness;* Edgar Wallace's *Sanders of the River* — these displayed the wide canvas of the European writer. Henry James, the American novelist, developed what critics called his "international theme" in *Daisy Miller, The Ambassadors, The Portrait of a Lady,* depicting the gaucheries of naïve Americans, among sophisticated Europeans. The European writer widened his literary canvas in writing science fiction. Jules Verne, the French fiction writer invaded the skies in the 1860s with *From the Earth to the Moon* predicting a journey to the moon from a rocket launched from Cape Canaveral. One hundred years later, man landed on the moon in a rocket launched from the same Cape Canaveral in the U. S. He further invaded the seas under the earth with *Twenty Thousand Leagues Under the Sea.* The American science fiction writer Alvin Toffler wrote

---

[15] Ibid.

Future Shock with his futuristic insistence that we should be "educating for change" that we should be `preparing people for the future" while warning that "unless man quickly learns to control the rate of change in his personal affairs, we are doomed to a massive adaptational breakdown."[16]

It becomes clear when one draws attention to the narrow canvas of the African writer in the twentieth century, busy as he was weeping over the losses inflicted on him by past colonial masters, preoccupied with blaming the African politician or military leaders for leading us into political and economic quagmire, that the time has come for a more forward-looking vision.

I have observed also that futuristic or utopian literature eluded the African writer in the twentieth century. African literature in the twentieth century, was so pre-occupied with what the French called *retour aux sources* (return to the sources) that writing imaginatively about the future eluded them. There was virtually no science fiction as I observed then (Inaugural 1114). Always looking imaginatively backward may have adversely affected Africa's developmental plans. Part of that lecture reads:

There are other uses of literature to which we have not called attention. Literature record man's infinite desire for the unattainable, for what Shelley calls, "the desire of the moth for a star." Man's longing for a perfect society, a society where all his problems have been solved, a paradise on earth, has bred a sub-genre of works popularly known as "Utopian Literature". Plato originated this sub-genre in the Greek words "Utopia" (no place) and Eutopia" (the good place in no place), giving it its generic nomenclature. In utopian literature, the wretched of the earth who unhappily find themselves in this valley of tears are invited to partake,

---

[16] Charles E. Nnolim. Inaugural Lecture University of Port Harcourt (July 13, 1988), 11 ff.

even if vicariously, of the kingdom idea, full of the delights and satisfactions denied them in this harsh world of reality. Utopian literature, therefore, is mainly a literature of escape because, the kernel of the sub-genre contains man's longing for a world where man's problems have already been solved and the tears of suffering humanity have completely been wiped dry.

Now, to deny that man needs promise of a better future to exist is to deny man's basic longing for a future of satisfactions and fulfilment — to pose hell for him instead of heaven, for all his deprivations, privations, hard work and struggles, and that would tantamount to denial of the truth of the essence of man's existence. We need utopian literature to fulfil man's anticipatory longing for a reward for his earthly kingdom into a heavenly kingdom." According to Paul Tillich (in "Critique and Justification of Utopia"), there are two main characteristics of utopia: its power and its fruitfulness. Its power builds on man's ontological discontent with his lot in life forcing man to break from this ontological discontent in order to transform his dreams into reality, and also its ability to open up possibilities for man which would have remained lost to him if not envisaged by utopian anticipation of human fulfilment.

The fruitfulness of utopia becomes the many realizations by man of his dreams on earth through his inventive genius and scientific discoveries that made possible a constantly dynamic present that keeps breaking into a better-realized future.

For those of us in the humane letters who read the bible as the Judaic literary legacy to the world, the Bible is utopian literature par excellence, depicting for mankind a visionary anticipation of the coming kingdom under God, the millennia at the end of time which is apocalyptic. By prophecy, by sheer intense if fanatical imaginative projection, the Israelites were able to break out from the slavery which was Egypt, to attainment of the Promised Land which was Jerusalem. The realization of the Jewish dream is proof of the power of utopia. Archibald Macleish had written in "America and Promises".

> America was always promises
> From the first voyage and the first ship
> There were promises.

And Bellamy in *Looking Backward* tells us:

> *Looking Backward* was written in the belief that the Golden Age lies before us and not behind us, and is not far away. Our Children shall surely see it, and we, too, who are already men and women, if we deserve it by our faith and by our work.

While science fiction which is, in the main, futuristic, crowds. Modern fiction-writing in Europe thus ensuring a more scientific, technologically-oriented future for Europe and the West, African utopia continues to be backward-looking. As Ivor Case puts it succinctly, in African traditional religions.

> There is no prophetism and no future paradise. For time... recedes rather than progresses and Golden Age — that era of the black man's greatness — the era of Timbuctoo and Benin, the era of the Yoruba and Zulu, of Shango and Chaka, lies in the Zamani period.
> The Sasa is an ever-constant construction of the past and not of the future. Utopia exists in the past ("Negritude and Utopianism" in inaugural p. 13)

The Negritude movement was African utopian literature par excellence with its consistent *retour aux sources* or return to-the sources theme. It was buttressed by the return to Africa movement of Marcus Garvey, the Harlem Renaissance in the U.S., Indigenism in Haiti, Afro-Cubanism in Cuba, the Rastafarian Movement in Jamaica, and the cult of primitivism in the Caribbean. Each, along with the Negritude movement was a *retour aux sources* romantic longing for African past by writers for whom Africa remained a lost paradise, to which we must all return for the authentication of our humanity denied, debased, and enslaved by the colonial masters. Alex Haley's *Roots* becomes in recent times, the enthronement of the ex-slave's longing for his place of origin. But nearer home, Chinua Achebe indulges in ancestor worship while Camara Laye returns imaginatively to his unspoilt childhood an unspoilt Guinea, while the most celebrated return syndrome in Caribbean literature is encapsulated is Cesaire's *Cahier d'un Retour au pays natal* (return to my native country).

As we can see, with all writers from Africa and African descent harping on return to the past, to the womb of time, where then is the shaping utopia for change in the future, for a future paradise where Africa's present problems are imaginatively solved? If it is true as Paul Tillich asserts, that "for a culture which has no utopia the present is inhibiting, the future holds no promise and the danger is very much there... of falling back to its past", aren't there great and disturbing implications for Africa, since we now recognize the fact that the power of utopia consists in its ability to transform dreams into reality? And since we further recognize that utopian literature, when it is futuristic and forward-looking has made inventions possible, what happens to us and to Africa where no anticipatory utopia exists to open up possibilities for man? Does this imply for us, as Paul Tillich suggests, "a sterile present" where "not only individual but cultural realization of human possibilities are inhibited and remain unfulfilled?"

The answer is not far to seek since we continue to send our best engineers and technologists to train in the effete factories in London when commonsense dictates that they trained in Japan whose innovative technology and technique of adapting other people's methods to suit her environment without destroying her culture, is the wonder of our modern technological age.

Since we, as Africans, do not project problems in the future and start to think of solving them now, it has not occurred to various African governments including our own to embark on a massive exposure of our engineers and scientists to the wonders of Japan so that we may learn how Japan maintains an enviably buoyant economy while it imports 100 per cent of its oil need and about 90 per cent of its steel requirement; how Japan has succeeded in beating the West at its own game. This lack of vision on our part has created enormous developmental problems for Africa.

I suggest that Africa's economic, developmental, and technological ills can only be cured by a proper infusion of the right sort of utopian literature in our midst, stranger than fiction as this may seem.

One of the thorniest issues confronting critics of African literature in the twentieth century is the problem of language. It was never fully resolved as the twenty-first century caught up with us. The use of European language, especially English and French by our major African writers is part of the inferiority complex displayed by our writers. Although a major writer like Ngugi Wa Thiong'o, had a dissenting voice, Achebe, Ayi Kwei Armah and Soyinka continue to write in English.

The use of language in African literature

When it comes to the use of language in African literature, the African creative writer's problem parallels that of his

European counterpart during the Renaissance. Both were confronted with the proper use of language (whether vernacular or foreign) in which to express oneself. Both the English and French writers of the Renaissance and their African counterparts in this century were the victims of a monumental hoax which forced both to suffer from an interiority complex about their vernacular.

In Renaissance Europe, a popular humanist theory insisted that "modern" dialects were the language of plebeians who spoke "vulgar" languages. In the belief that the ancients had used superior language, Greek and Latin, Francis Bacon, not trusting the survival of the English tongue, had most of his works translated into Latin, and Roger Ascham complained in *Toxophilus* (1544), which was grudgingly written in English, that "to have written this book either in Latin or Greek... had been much easier." Mulcaster, another English contemporary of Ascham, began a campaign for other English writers to use the English language because English was "the joyful title of our liberty and freedom, the Latin tongue remembering us of our thraldom" — a passage that every African literature artist should paste on his typewriter.

Du Bellay in his *Defence et illustration de langue francaise* (1549), appealing to the nationalistic sentiments of his fellow Frenchmen, had argued that French people were as good as the Romans or any other people, ancient or modern, and that it was the patriotic duty of every Frenchman to write in French and thus enrich it with his learning — another *vade mecum* that is urged on our African writers.

The African writer of today who churns out masterpieces in a foreign language must be reminded of two things. First, one must draw his attention to Dante and Petrarch and Boccaccio. What made Dante a world famous writer who takes his stand by the immortals, are not his writings in Latin, e.g. *De Vulgari Eloquentia* but *the Divine Comedy* written in his 'vulgar' Florentine. Boccaccio's *Decameron* and Petrarch's sonnets — all were written in the vulgar tongue, even though these writers in the vulgar tongue, even though these writers were highly educated in Greek and Latin. By lending the weight of their authority to the vernacular, these writers brought authority and dignity to bear on their native Italian and thus catapulted it into a language worthy of world recognition. This is a healthy nationalism in the use of language in literary expression.

The other thing the African writer must bear in mind is that throughout literary history no writer has been proved great who insists on talking to his own people through an interpreter — via a foreign tongue. The African writer must understand that the only way to internationalize African languages will be to write in them, thus lending their authority and prestige to these languages.

To assume a language one critic has remarked, is to assume a worldview. The African writer who writes in a foreign tongue must understand that yelling curses back at Prospero in Prospero's own tongue is half the story and a misguided idea at that. According to George Lamming, provided there is no extraordinary departure which explodes all of Prospero's premises, then Caliban and his future now belong to Prospero... Prospero lives in the absolute certainty that Language, which is his gift to Caliban, is the very prison in which Caliban's achievements will be realized and restricted.[17]

The tragedy of our era is that our African writers not only imprison themselves in the language of their masters but physically imprison themselves in the very land of their

---

[17] George Lamming, *The Pleasures of Exile* (London, 1960), 109.

enslavers for the paltry glitter of the enslaver's money. Prospero, of course, very cunning and self-effacing, laughs up his sleeves, confident that whatever the African achieves in the way of literary art would only be derivative and as long as it remains in Prospero's language, it would continue to show the latter's continuing stranglehold.

An important difference then is that while the English or French writer during the Renaissance recognized his imprisonment and thraldom as he wrote in a foreign language and did something about it, the African writer recognizes his bondage only does nothing about it but incomprehensibly hugs it more tightly to his breast.[18]

One definite accomplishment of African pioneer writers in the twentieth century is the establishment of the African tradition in literature, that tradition which highlights the African world view. It is that tradition which makes creative use of our local proverbs, legends, folk tales and local myths in giving expression to what is indigenous in African culture.

On the Nigerian literary scene, Tutuola first comes to mind in the creative use of our mythologies. His *Palm Wine Drinkard and My Life in the Bush of Ghosts* belong to a world of fantasy and superstition. Tutuola experiments with ethnic Yoruba myths which he built into a private mythopoeia. We give Tutuola the credit for being the first Nigerian to "Africanize" the English language and domesticate it for local use in fiction. We further give Tutuola the credit as a writer who represents the transition from our oral to the written transition.[19]

We have established that Achebe is the inaugurator of

---

[18] For this Section on the use of Language in African Literature, please see Charles E. Nnolim, An African Literary Aesthetic: A Prolegomenon Ba Shiru, vol. 7, No. 2 (1976), 68-70.

[19] Eustace Palmer. *The Growth of the African Novel.* London: Heinemann (1978), 34.

the great tradition in African literature. He owes to Tutuola the Africanization of the English language, the "bending" of the English language to suit local expressions and mannerisms. But first and foremost, Achebe is concerned with cultural assertion and is a pioneer in what has come to be called cultural nationalism in African literature especially in re-establishing the "African personality" and emphasizing the dignity of the black man and woman. Achebe does this exceptionally well by making creative use of our folk tradition, the delightful turns of our proverbs, the respect for our ancestors, what critics refer to as ancestor worship, plus promotion of what is best in the art of story, garnished with the charm of our folkways, crowned with the rehabilitation of the dignity of the black man bruised and damaged by the colonial masters.

And what Achebe did was done so well that other African writers whom he anticipated so well, had no option but to copy him. We now discuss the legacy of Achebe, his "sons" and "daughters" who consciously or unconsciously tried to imitate him both in Nigeria and in the Diaspora: Elechi Amadi, Onuora Nzekwu, Flora Nwapa, Ngugi Wa Thiong'o, John Munonye, Ayi Kwei Armah.

In the African tradition in literature, Cyprian Ekwensi blazed a different trail. He is the father of the urban novel, owing a lot to the Onitsha Market pamphlet literature. If Achebe's *Things Fall Apart* and Amadi's *The Concubine* are are examples of the rural novel, Ekwensi's *People of the City* and *Jagua Nana* are are examples of the city or urban novel.

Ekwensi is Nigeria's novelist of the city chronicling life in our urban environments. Ekwensi is a pioneer in his own right. He is excited by the prostitute, the crooked politician, the political thug, the sex maniac, fallen men and women fighting to establish their identities in a terribly wicked world. What energizes Ekwensi's characters, the compelling principle in their lives is money, sex, crime, power, politics. Ekwensi is also credited with establishing the picaresque tradition in African literature: the tradition of the migrant from the village to the city and from place to place within the city. And Cyprian Ekwensi "legitimized" the use of Pidgin English in African literature. Ekwensi had his own "sons", writers in the tradition of the Macmillan "pacesetters" series, who, like Ekwensi wrote to a pre-set formula, whose output degenerated to para-literature, long on mass appeal, short on artistic depth. Both Ekwensi and his "sons", introduced popular literature in African fiction.

Finally, this study has established that literature and its attendant criticism have marked epochal landmarks in National Development in the history of Nigeria in the twentieth century. Chinua Achebe's NNMA lecture: "What Has Literature Got to Do With It: "had an eye on the part that literature plays in our" national life and national development. The writer acts as the weather vane to the critic and this study equally calls attention to the part criticism plays in national development as it helps to shape that literature. Achebe was the first Nigerian writer to be awarded the Nigerian National Merit Award (NNMA) for excellence. Since I am not a "writer" in the classic sense of creative writing but a critic of "writers", I take some pride in suspecting that I was awarded the honour as the first Nigerian critic, as a man of letters who has never published a novel or a play or a book of poetry. For the letter informing me of the nomination said:

> This is in recognition of your unique and outstanding contributions to scholarship and research which has contributed in no small way to national development in the field of humanities. (Signed Adamu Bawa Mu' azu Secretary, (NNMA)

Index

Printed in the United States
By Bookmasters